Emotional Crises

BY DR. PETER H. STEVENS

ODYSSEY PRESS • NEW YORK

ACKNOWLEDGMENTS

I owe special thanks to Mrs. Sybil Taylor. The completion of this book would have been impossible without her help, her sound editorial judgment, and—last but not least— her infinite patience with the "emotional crises" that occur in connection with the writing of a book.

I am also deeply indebted to Miss Helen K. Katz who has been of invaluable assistance in typing, revising, and rewriting some of the presented material. She has given generously of her time and I am grateful for her many constructive suggestions.

P.H.S.

TABLE OF CONTENTS

A WORD FROM THE AUTHOR / How Psychology
Can Help
in Emotional Crises

What are the first ideas that come to your mind when you hear
the word emergency? Perhaps you think of an accident, a fire, a
bodily injury, or a threat to your life. How fortunate you are to
be protected against such crises by emergency first aid stations
in hospitals, elaborately equipped fire departments, and medical
first aid kits in your home or office.

However, the emergency situations described so far are
caused by the external environment, and are mainly concerned
with threats to your physical health. Where can you find quick
and effective emergency aid when your mental or emotional
balance is upset? For instance: you are under pressure to make
a vital decision or choice; your marriage is about to break up; you
suddenly realize how alone you are in this world, and that nobody seems to care whether you live or die; or you fear you will
break down on a job that you can't handle. Though emergencies
of this kind may not pose an immediate threat to your physical
health, your experience of them may be as painful as the ache
of a heart attack or the agony of a broken leg. What can you do
to alleviate the immediate pain? Can a knowledge of psychology
help you in situations of this kind? If so, how can it be applied
to some of the major crises of our lives?

In the past psychologists have given only scant attention

to the topic of emotional first aid. Perhaps because they thought that premature and overly hasty aid in emotional crises may be more damaging than no help at all. To be sure, such an attitude was justified when psychological knowledge was in its infancy and when there was little scientific theory to support concrete advice and recommendations. This situation, however, no longer holds true for this day and age.

Though a precise knowledge of the complex anatomy of our personality make-up still lags in comparison with the findings of the "exact" natural sciences, extended research and wider clinical experience have placed the whole field of psychology on a more firmly established basis. For instance: various psychological defense mechanisms which we unwittingly employ in order to escape emotional pain and injury have been isolated and defined. The way in which hostility and fear can twist our best efforts to come to terms with our problems has been delineated quite specifically. That distorted attitudes of the past can play tricks with us in the present has been more clearly recognized. With such insight into these and other dynamic aspects of human behavior, should it not be possible to apply this knowledge when it is most needed—during the emotional crises and emergencies of life?

It is, of course, impossible to prescribe psychological first aid remedies that completely eradicate emotional suffering. Though the authors of some popular psychology books claim that they can provide the key to everlasting happiness "in ten easy lessons," their common sense suggestions are often not much different from the advice of a next-door neighbor or friend (notwithstanding the fact that such books are phrased in a psychological jargon that is very impressive to the layman). While it may be upsetting to contemplate the fact that such experiences as anger, fear, guilt, and apprehension are probably inevitable parts of living, nobody has yet devised a quick rule of thumb by which they can be entirely eliminated.

Though it is true then that life can never be a bed of roses, I believe, nevertheless, that the characteristic attitudes with which we approach our psychological crises are subject to change. Psychologists usually refer to such attitudes as "defense" or "adjustment" mechanisms. In order to show you their significance, let me outline some of those that occur with particular frequency in situations of emotional stress.

First, when confronted with an emergency, we are inclined to *overdefend* ourselves, acting much like an automobile with an overly sensitive brake system. Or we *underdefend* ourselves, being similar in this respect to an alarm clock that always rings *after* the crucial hour for which it has been set. (Though the underdefender's caution will lead him at times to practice good judgment in some situations, more often his excessive restraint will render him helpless in emergencies.)

Secondly, in coping with new crises we are bound to lean too much and too exclusively on *past experience*. We do this almost automatically, not realizing that every new situation is different and calls for a unique kind of readjustment. For example, the man who always got his way by throwing a temper tantrum as a child will be unable as an adult to settle a marital crisis by the discussion method.

A third detrimental inclination in stress situations is the tendency to *project* our anger toward the most readily available recipient instead of toward the cause of the trouble. Thus, the wife who is frustrated by her husband's lack of attention may hit her child to release her frustration.

Finally, under duress, *we try to hide like ostriches,* hoping that a state of apathy and oblivion will be our best protection against impending emergencies.

These are, of course, just a few of the detrimental ways in which we try to fend off disaster at times of emotional stress. That such ways of defending ourselves in critical situations could be brought under more effective conscious control is suggested by the fact that we usually realize quite clearly *after* an emotional crisis has passed how "idiotic" and "thickskulled" was our behavior. During the emergency situation, it is as though some powerful unconscious force blinds us to the necessary action. It is only after the situation is over that the mind sees clearly what *should* have been done. Then a sort of hindsight develops which, however, usually occurs too late.

Can such hindsight ever be replaced by foresight? I think so, and to aid you to do so is precisely one of the goals of this book. The book attempts to strip your mind of the many childish, irrelevant, irrational, and inappropriate impulses that stultify you when you are confronted with an emotional crisis. At the same time, it makes an endeavor to focus your attention on those thoughts and feelings that are effective in overcoming an emergency situation. Why our best and most constructive impulses seem to desert us under emotional duress is not yet known. Nevertheless, it seems clear that we need reassurance and encouragement in order to recognize and accept our best impulses and intuitions. It is hoped that the reader will get help of this kind from this book.

I began the book with the section "Crises Within Yourself" because I believe that internal conflicts strongly influence our reactions to external crises, and also because such emotional pressures from within can often be more devastating than those from without.

Although I do not subscribe to the notion of a death instinct in the strict sense of the word, I do believe that all of us have self-destructive tendencies that threaten to take over in situations of stress. Learning how to cope with such impulses when immediate psychiatric help is not available is one of the purposes of the chapters which are included in the first section.

The second section deals with emergencies that are thrust upon us *suddenly* and call for some kind of immediate remedial action. Some of the situations which will be discussed involve the experience of severe loss, of being cut off from a previous source of emotional security and support. The person who has lost a loved one, who is confronted by divorce, who finds himself suddenly unemployed, or who is confronted with the exigencies of unwanted pregnancy, is in dire need of emotional help and practical advice. True, the conditions which cause such crises are often irreversible. However, there are always things that can be done to alter the approach to such situations. I have tried to suggest those remedial measures that I have found most helpful in dealing with some of my patients.

When you read the section of this book entitled "Troubled Relationships" you may be reminded of the many books and articles that are concerned with "how to make friends and how to get along with people." The emphasis in my book will not be on how to become more "popular" in a superficial way, but on how to deal with crises in *close* relationships. That these so often constitute "emergencies" (instead of a source of emotional support and mental comfort) becomes more clear if we realize that being emotionally close to others may lead to exposure of our innermost fears, faults, and areas of hypersensitivity. It is likely that this section about the more intimate phases of your social life, and the crises connected with it, will be of special concern to you.

In my treatment of "Parent-Child Crises" I have steered away from putting too much emphasis on how to raise and educate children—a topic that has been widely covered in books by pediatricians, child psychologists, and child psychiatrists. I thought it would be more helpful to talk about those problems that arise when there is friction between adults and their parents. Though such friction is quite common, its causes have rarely been taken up in articles on parent-child relationships. Another topic that has been given only scant attention in psychological literature is the anxiety that is often experienced by mothers after childbirth. Since such anxiety is not an uncommon experience, I believe that a discussion of the psychological aspects of this situation should not be omitted from a section on parent-child crises.

The book ends with the section "Helping Others in Emotional Trouble"; for, if we begin by solving our own internal problems, we may end by giving aid to others. Vital crises arise often *when others in emotional distress seek our advice and reassurance.* Whether we like it or not, life forces many of us to play the role of the amateur psychotherapist. A mere confirmatory nodding of our heads or a derogatory silence may often exert a powerful influence on someone who is disturbed. I don't believe, of course, that the layman should try to practice psychotherapy. In fact, I think that this could be quite dangerous. Nevertheless, whatever aid the amateur confidant may dispense to the emotionally troubled could be sharpened and refined by acquiring knowledge of some of the basic principles and techniques of professional psychotherapy, and it is to aid you in acquiring these that this section was written.

In conclusion I'd like to raise two points which may have occurred to you while you were reading the previous statements. First, you may already be aware of several of the considerations offered so far on the basis of your own life experience. Don't let this disturb you! For it is confirmation and verification of your most constructive thoughts and feelings that you need most urgently at times of emotional duress, and there is little to be gained from ideas and suggestions that do not touch at least some familiar chord in you. Second, the emergency situations set forth here leave out many important events, and thus comprise only a tiny sample of the urgent emotional predicaments that we run into daily. I believe, however, that if you can combat the aforementioned emotional crises and can fight them with a somewhat sharpened psychological insight, you will be better off and the reading of this book will not have been a waste of time and energy.

PART ONE

Crises

Within

Yourself

CHAPTER 1 /

Fear of
A Nervous Breakdown

"Doctor, I must see you right away. I just can't take it any more. I think I'm on the verge of a nervous breakdown. I'm shaky all over and—you'll probably laugh—but I think I'm losing my mind. I make stupid mistakes on the job; the phone rings and I'm so jumpy, I could hit the ceiling; I hear a love song over the radio and I could start bawling like a five-year-old kid! What's wrong with me? You just have to see me, or I don't know what I may do!"

This is a verbatim account of a telephone call from a woman patient who had reached her emotional breaking point. Perhaps you too have felt like this at times, and have been plagued by fleeting, nagging doubts about your mental "normality" or emotional stability.

Worry about incipient insanity can sometimes be traced to the presence of one single fear. Such was the case with one of my patients whom I shall call John.

With his bright sports jacket and his devil-may-care attitude, John gave the impression of being a person without out a worry in the world. However, he suffered from a most serious problem. Each time he entered a subway tunnel, he was seized by uncontrollable panic and he felt —these are his own words—"as if the subway tunnel were going to close in on me and I was going to be crushed under its weight." He was a bright and very reasonable fellow otherwise, and he realized that it was eccentric to have such fears. Nevertheless, when these states of panic overcame him, he lost all control over himself, and was convinced that he would end up in a mental institution.

In addition to people who believe themselves "crazy" because they are plagued by abnormal fears, there are countless others who doubt their sanity because of what they have read in psychology books, or heard in lectures. Since we live in an age which puts much faith in psychology, and since knowledge of this kind is easily available to the public, the layman is prone to identify too quickly with whatever psychiatric case history bears the slightest resemblance to his own troubled state of mind.

Suppose you become depressed as the result of an accumulation of upsetting experiences, or you find that you lose interest in everything—in your appearance, in your hobbies, in your friends. You try to pay attention to your work, but careless errors that you have never made before creep in. More than that, you believe that your memory is slipping at times, and you are absent-minded when you talk with people. You read in a psychology book about loss of memory, symptoms of withdrawal, loss of contact with reality, and "schizophrenia." Would it not be quite easy for you to assume that perhaps you too are in the early stages of what is sometimes called a "split personality," or that you are a "manic-depressive"?

The fear of becoming one of those who end up behind the gates of a mental institution is also reinforced if there is or has been mental disturbance in the family background. Perhaps you have an aunt or a distant relative who has received shock treatment, or who ended life by sudden suicide as the result of a depression. How easy it is for you now to think that your future fate may be similar to that of the disturbed relative.

If thoughts and ideas of this kind bother you frequently, or even enter your mind occasionally, your apprehension and worry can be greatly relieved by learning some of the facts that scientists have established in connection with such concepts as insanity, abnormality, and emotional disturbances.

Most research workers in the field of psychiatry and psychology are very dubious about the hereditary basis for most mental disturbances. The fact that someone in your family was emotionally ill does not indicate that such a disturbance will be passed on to you in the same manner in which you inherit eye color or other physical characteristics. The exact causes of so-called insanity are still largely unknown, and even less is known about its hereditary manifestations. In fact, there is evidence that it is not an inherited trait. Emotionally healthy and well-balanced children have sometimes been the offspring of parents whose own mental health has been impaired.

The very fact that you are so anxious and concerned about your emotional imbalance is a favorable sign, for this reason: the majority of individuals who "lose their minds" are usually *not* anxious about their mental state. In fact, they may deny any trouble vehemently, even if emotional disturbance is suspected by others. Thus, your worry and anxiety about your own mental state could be looked at as a healthy *defense,* just as the body develops its own antibodies to fight infection and illness.

Quite a few individuals who fear insanity are actually experiencing essentially normal emotions and sensations, only *they are temporarily magnified under a situation of stress.* All of us "lose our minds" *temporarily* when we are angry and upset. Thus, the person who is jilted in love may have the illusion that his world has come to an end. Similarly, the individual who is temporarily depressed may surmise that happiness has gone out of his life forever.

Most psychotherapists agree that "abnormality" is a vague and arbitrarily defined concept. At any rate, because you have abnormal thoughts and wishes at times is no reason for labeling yourself a "psycho." Take this situation: perhaps you have always conceived of yourself as being *different* because you had to get much of your real satisfaction from a world of fantasy and make-believe. Possibly you found that you could not get really close to people and that there was always an insurmountable wall that separated you from another person. Or, you may have experienced rejection and indifference when you tried to put your best foot forward and attempted to convey warmth and affection. Such feelings and experiences do not necessarily turn you into a psychiatric case, as long as you are able to *compensate for them in a manner that is not destructive to yourself or others.*

If you are afraid of mental disturbance, try to conceive of the human mind as something that is extremely flexible and quite strong and capable of taking many hard knocks. You have heard about individuals who were tortured in concentration camps, exposed to the horrors of war, injured seriously and, as a result, lost almost all that was precious to them. But consider that many of those survivors made an excellent recovery. It is of course true that all of us have a potential emotional breaking point. Our inherent capacity to endure emotional pain and agony is, however, usually far greater than we think. People who do break down emotionally are like swimmers who have the strength to save themselves in dangerous waters, but drown because their anxiety makes them lose bodily control.

If your anxiety is so intense that you are worried about an emotional breakdown in public (perhaps in the form of a crying spell), make sure that an anticipated "attack" is not an unconscious bid for attention and sympathy. Though we seem to dread sickness and helplessness, secretly we often love and enjoy the attention it can bring. That is why a crutch or a prominently displayed bandage can have a pleasant, attention-getting value, and there are many patients who will therefore continue to use these implements long after they are needed. Likewise, a publicly displayed nervous breakdown may be your unconscious device for calling attention to your problems. It could also be a devious and hostile way for getting even with those who have been indifferent to your troubles in the past. If you note such tendencies in yourself, remember that the attention and sympathy which is attained this way is often short-lived, may not be genuine, and can ruin other people's respect for you.

The suggestions offered so far are an appeal to your reason and judgment. The following are some more practical hints on what to *do:*

No matter how upset you feel, *try to continue with some of your daily chores and keep on working.* If you stay by yourself now and try to analyze intellectually what really has an emotional basis, you may only plunge yourself more deeply into despair and confusion. Contact with other people on a job, or the satisfaction derived from even minor duties, may draw your attention away from yourself.

If you feel that you *must* see a psychotherapist right away, go ahead. However, realize that most psychotherapists have a schedule of appointments which render them rarely available for emergency consultations. There are emergency psychiatric clinics in larger cities that may be better equipped to help you, if you need aid in a hurry. (See appendix for the best method of locating one.)

If you think that a psychological expert can detect the basic source of your emotional trouble and remedy it in *one visit,* you will be disappointed. Obviously the causes for breakdowns and emotional crises are complex and of long standing, and their exploration usually takes considerable time. What you can expect from an initial contact with a psychotherapist is genuine attention and empathy, and the kind of relief that comes from talking out your troubles in the presence of a professionally qualified individual. In addition, the feeling of having taken

13

action toward combating what bothers you may be helpful.

It is possible that talking to a friend about your fear of insanity may be all that you want to do for the time being. However, keep in mind one important consideration: select the person to whom you decide to unburden yourself *very carefully*. It should be someone whom you really trust and respect—someone who has been helpful to you in similar situations in the past. Consulting your niece who has taken an introductory psychology course in college, or writing to "Dear Abby" would probably be wrong.

You may, on the other hand, be the kind of person who is made to feel worse by talking to others about your emotional dilemmas. It may hurt your pride deeply to confess your troubles to others and thus destroy the image of yourself as a strong and self-sufficient person. Before you consult others, you might be able to regain your emotional composure in solitude and by wise and honest consultation with your inner self.

CHAPTER **2** / Fear of

Aging

NEW IDEAS ABOUT OLD AGE

People used to worry about old age when they approached their sixties, seventies, or eighties. Today, however, the girl who has not found a husband while in her twenties is developing an old-age complex. Similarly, the young man who has not become a junior executive in his thirties is beginning to lie about the date of his birth on application blanks.

A chapter which is concerned with problems of old age must therefore be directed to a much wider age group, though most of the suggestions offered here will apply somewhat more to people at or about retirement age.

If you feel, then, that your years are beginning to show on you, if you become rather anxious because you fear life is slipping by too quickly and you are not getting enough out of it, there are several things that you can do to push back "psychological old age." Here they are:

Don't envy youth. It is often harder to be young than to be old. Though young people supposedly have the world open to them, and are said to have unlimited opportunities ahead, the uncertainty of their futures is more often a source of anxiety than a reason for joyful anticipation. Moreover, young people frequently are not aware of their advantages (greater strength, beauty, agility) and therefore take them for granted.

Also, it is not true that youth is a period of greater freedom. If you are getting on in years now, you are in many ways much more free and independent, for young people are at the mercy of their (often highly critical) parents and teachers, who curtail their freedom of action a great deal of the time.

You may envy young people because they often have stronger sex drives. But young persons are not as free in expressing their sex drives, and are often more bewildered and confused about them than older individuals.

Live more in the present than in the past. The tendency to regress is not confined to the period of old age, though it crops up more frequently as we grow older and are inclined to look backward instead of forward.

Nothing is more annoying to others and more certain to kill interest than recourse to the good old days. Do you want to be considered very old? Then just make comments like these: "When I was a child . . . That reminds me of a story that I heard a long time ago. . . . That is exactly what happened to me when I was sick so many years ago. . . . I have always done it this way in the past and I am not going to change now. . . ." You may have such thoughts in your mind, but expressing them will add at least ten years to your age in the opinion of others.

To counteract the aging process, adopt at least one new idea every month, break at least one old established habit every week, and do something that you have never done before every other day. A difficult prescription to follow, but it could do more for counteracting old age than having your face lifted, or getting a youthful tan at your barber's.

Slow motion is strongly associated with old age in people's minds. Watch a meeting of the senior board of directors of a business organization, and then look at a gathering of Boy Scouts. The difference in motility between the two groups reflects the discrepancy between age and youth. Therefore, if you want to appear young to others, in fact, want to *feel* young, try to move just a little faster than you have lately been used to (without, of course, overstraining yourself to a point where it interferes with your health). However, speed is not confined to physical motion. Try to be more quick in grasping new ideas, and to express yourself with less restraint and more gusto and enthusiasm.

Watch for the reappearance of old neurotic traits in new disguise. As the years add up, you may get the feeling that you don't command quite the same respect and attention that you used to. As a result, you may try to adjust to this crisis by unconsciously exaggerating some of your neurotic characteristics.

Were you perhaps something of a miser in the past? Then you'll become even more stingy now and exaggerate the save-all trait, pinching pennies whenever you can. Were you a little bit on the bossy side previously? Did you shout your way to success? Make sure the hidden "boss" in you is not growing into a tyrant as you become older. Did feelings of inadequacy make you overly dependent upon others during childhood and adolescence? As you push on in years, the same old feeling of helplessness could come back with greater force. Soon you'll come to think that the world, and especially those close to you, now owe you that extra amount of attention which you never received before. As a result of such exaggerated traits, you could become more obnoxious with every day that you grow older.

Therefore, become more conscious of these neurotic tendencies—how they can grow more extreme with the aging process—and you'll avoid many crises of later life.

Try to make new friends instead of depending primarily upon already established ones and family connections. One of the big problems of the aging person is, of course, loneliness. This feeling is enhanced if the individual involved clings tenaciously to old friends and family members, perhaps gradually losing initiative for new and different social experiences.

If you as an aging person notice even the slightest tendency in this direction, you must realize that this is "murder" for you. Your old friends should be appreciated and enjoyed; however, if you associate with them exclusively, your ideas and points of view will also remain old and unchanged, and you'll age prematurely. Keep in touch with what is current and exciting in the world today.

If you are a widow or widower, think twice before you move in with your children, especially if they are middle-aged and married. Don't become too dependent upon them economically, emotionally, or in any other way. To lean exclusively on others during old age is a great temptation; and it offers many *surface* advantages, particularly if your strength, health, and earning powers are waning. However, it rarely pays off in the long run. There will be times when your state of dependency will make you feel hostile against those who support you, because the situation only emphasizes how weak and helpless you really are.

Seek the company of young people, and you will stay young. There is no better way to push back the horrors of getting old than to keep in touch with the young generation. However, you must know how to go about it. If you approach young people with the idea of teaching and indoctrinating them with your ideas, or if you try to impress them with your superior knowledge and experience, you can easily become a bore to them. However, if you can put yourself in their place and try to listen to and to understand them rather than to preach and to reform, you will never lose rapport with them. Wise and genuinely understanding older people have rarely been at a loss for youthful company. If young people yawn, or if they try to avoid you, the fault is probably your attitude, not your more advanced age.

Don't give up looking for love, but learn to enjoy it in a different way. One of the saddest and most difficult things for the person who gets older to accept is that the kind of love which is based mainly on sex and romance occurs less frequently, or not at all. This is a particularly bitter pill to swallow since sexual needs and desires often seem to outlast our capacities.

I would even go so far as to say that about ninety per cent of all anxiety about getting old is essentially a fear of losing love, affection, or sexual attraction. Just how many people would want to go on a diet, have more youthful skin, or wear a toupee if it were not to appear more attractive to members of the opposite sex? Very few, if any, I believe.

If people fall in love with you as an older person, it may be more *because* of your personality than *in spite* of it.

Most of us have a deep need to be appreciated for our sex performance, and disappointment along these lines has marred the happiness of many aging people. How can this be prevented? You can deceive yourself by acting younger than you are, pretending and chasing men or women as if you were in your teens. If you have prestige, money, and some charm, you may fool yourself and others, at least for a while; but a feeling of emptiness and disappointment will eventually spoil the fun. A better way of adjusting to the loss of appeal with advancing years may be this: realize that sex without love is actually short-lived. Instead, affection, genuine respect, admiration, and real closeness are lasting and important ingredients of love. They form the core of any relationship—whether you are old or young. Why not concentrate on binding love in this way?

Love rarely comes to you in the exact manner in which you desire it. It may take the form of affectionate friendship when you crave a more emotional entanglement. But then, is affection not better than loneliness and an old age that is devoid of *any* kind of love?

CHAPTER 3 / Fear of Retirement

The Webster dictionary defines retirement as a state of retreat, and the word "retire" is described as "to put away, to withdraw from circulation or from the market." In view of the essentially negative associations that we form upon hearing the word retirement, it is not surprising that the prospect of being retired often arouses shock and fear, rather than joyful anticipation.

In their advertisements, some life insurance companies depict an aged man or a retired couple smiling gaily and looking extremely carefree. Seeing these ads, you may wonder just how happy or unhappy *you* are going to feel when you receive your "walking papers."

Though some people do not relish the thought of retirement, there are certain advantages connected with it. Some of these advantages are: (1) You are not tied down to a job anymore and thus are more free to move away and start a new life in a different community. (2) Retirement may make it possible for you to travel and to see places you have never visited before. (3) You may find some *new* kind of employment which could be more interesting and satisfying than the work you were engaged in before you retired. Let us consider these advantages and see if they can be utilized to make your days of retirement more enjoyable.

MOVING TO A NEW COMMUNITY

This step may be especially advisable if you have many outdoor hobbies. It may now be practical as well as desirable to move from an urban area to a place where you are able to indulge in fishing, hunting, swimming, or any number of sports. States such as Florida and California are ideal locations in which to establish an outdoor life, and it is probably for this reason, as well as for sunshine, that many people who have retired from work like to live there. However, before you consider such a step, realize that you are moving to a geographical area that is literally flooded with other retired people. Though there undoubtedly are certain advantages when "birds of a feather flock together," you may prefer to move to a region that also brings you in contact with younger people who are not retirees.

Of course, you may not want to move from the neighborhood that is familiar to you and where you have many friends. On the other hand, changing the environment to which you have grown so accustomed and starting a new life somewhere else, may make retirement more interesting and enjoyable.

SATISFYING THE URGE TO TRAVEL

Now is the time when you can satisfy a life-long ambition to travel and to see the world. Don't be afraid of the cost, or fearful that a trip will dig too deeply into your financial resources. Though everybody seems to be out for your dollar when you travel as a tourist, your situation as a retired man or woman is slightly different. Unlike the person who is traveling on a short vacation, you can save money by taking your trips during the off-seasons, when transportation and hotel rates drop considerably. Also, you can travel at a somewhat more leisurely pace than the vacationer who has to be back on the job. You can spend more time at the places you visit, and thus have an opportunity to get acquainted with the people of those places. Making friends will give you someone to visit the next time, and will help you escape hotel life.

21

However, let me sound one note of warning: traveling by yourself can be lonely at times. Even if you have the adventurous spirit of a Marco Polo, there may be times when you feel "rootless" in different communities, and such a feeling can make you painfully aware of the less pleasant aspects of retirement. To anticipate and avoid such moments, it may be wise to travel to places where you already have friends or where you have social introductions. Another way of combating travel-loneliness may be to join one of the tours that are especially planned by travel agencies for single people or retired couples. Joining a group of this kind may raise your travel expenses to some extent; nevertheless, the additional cost is a worthwhile investment if it can prevent future loneliness.

FINDING A NEW JOB AFTER RETIREMENT FROM WORK

Provided that you are in good health, you may want to continue working—either on a full- or part-time basis. You may wish to seek a new type of employment or perhaps remain at the work you have been doing all along.

Start to think about the kind of retirement job best suited for you long before *the day of your retirement comes.* For whether you want to operate a chicken farm, or become a nurse for babies, your future goals will take some preparation and some investigation of the prevailing opportunities in the field you wish to enter. You should go about preparing yourself for your vocational life after fifty or sixty just as seriously as though you were a young boy who knows he will have to enter some occupational field when he graduates from school. If you know before you retire just what kind of work is ahead of you and have already taken steps toward preparing yourself for it, you will not be a victim of "retirement blues."

Of course, if you like the work that you have been doing all along, and find the opportunity to continue it on your own, or on a part-time basis, you are fortunate. In fact, you might now enjoy doing this work even more because you are under less pressure and can do it at your own pace. This situation may hold true, for instance, if you are a writer, a scientist, a research man, or have been in business for yourself. The problem is somewhat more difficult if you have been indifferent to your past job or have even *hated* it. Now, however, you can engage in work that you like and that gives you real job satisfaction and a minimum of vocational headaches. It is in instances like these that you may find the services of an experienced vocational counselor or psychologist most helpful.

Make a very careful analysis of your past hobbies and try to use this as a starting point for a new job. Though your hobbies may not *seem* to be marketable, there may be some way for you to convert them into profitable skills.

> Some time ago a retired bank officer consulted me. His only hobby was sailing, and he did not know how he could make any occupational use of it now. I suggested that he explore the opportunities for becoming a salesman of boats and yachts. Because of his age he was unable to get such a job, but the contacts that he made while applying to various boat-building companies finally led to employment as a cruise manager operating chartered boats for others. His knowledge of boating was not as useless as he had thought before he took steps to explore the prevailing opportunities.

Are you very fond of animals? Do you love dogs, cats, tropical fish, or canaries? You may have brushed such interest aside in connection with a post-retirement career. However, I myself was surprised to find that a love for the animal world can be utilized vocationally by opening a pet shop, or by operating a kennel that boards animals over the weekend and when people are on vacations. Are you fond of music and play an in-

23

strument? You could try to *teach* music. Have you collected stamps or coins? There are people who derive a major source of income from this. Therefore, a careful scrutiny of your past and present hobbies may be the way to find a new vocation.

Make an attempt to get work that involves at least some financial return and is not voluntary or unpaid. The fact that a job is worthwhile enough to involve financial expenditure on the part of your employer adds to its significance—in your eyes and in the eyes of other people. This is particularly essential for the retired person who needs to feel that whatever he has to contribute in the way of work is valued and recognized. Perhaps it is unfortunate, but we can't get away from the fact that the feeling of job success and achievement is somehow tied up with the price others put on it. Therefore, the retired man or woman should turn to voluntary and unpaid work only after all possibilities for remunerative employment have been explored.

Try not to work alone. Select a job that keeps you in contact with others. Among the pleasures of work are the social contacts that it facilitates. Who would want to work in complete isolation? Very few people. This held true before you retired from work, and it is even more true now that you are looking for new employment. Therefore, if you decide to engage in work that isolates you from others most of the time, you may experience a strong sense of loneliness and uselessness.

This is what happened to a woman who had to retire from her job as a teacher and was trying to fill the now empty hours of her previous working days by writing science fiction stories. Her new solitary work made her miss the social stimulation of her former teaching position, and she became very depressed. She gladly followed my suggestion to look for employment that kept her in touch with other people at least part of the time. Tutoring, giving lessons in remedial reading, and helping with clerical work in the local library proved more satisfactory to her than trying to write fiction in the confines of her home.

Anticipate and try to counteract employers' prejudices against your age. You might just as well face it—some prejudice against the older individual does exist in the employment world. Though you may look ten or even twenty years younger than you are, and though you may move faster than the youngest office boy or secretary in an organization, your age may be held against you. It is sometimes a latent fear of parental domination that makes younger people hesitate to hire the older job applicant. Possibly they fear competition with you because of your greater experience. But the fact remains that you will encounter discrimination. How can you cope with this situation?

(1) *Apply for the job in person.* Don't apply by letter. For if a prospective employer speaks with you and gets to know you, he may overlook the numerals on your application blank and notice how psychologically young you are, and how quickly you act and comprehend.

(2) *Try to convince your prospective employer that you are a good employment "buy."* You can make certain work adjustments that younger employees find harder to comply with. For example, you are more ready to work evening hours or to put in some extra time on weekends or holidays. Since employment opportunities are scarce at your age, the chances are you won't be absent from work as often as younger employees; you'd think twice before taking a day off because of some personal business that you want to attend to. And, although you might be more susceptible to minor illnesses than a younger person, you would still hesitate to stay home from work.

If you are a married woman and beyond the childbearing age, there would be no harm in suggesting subtly that the danger of your quitting or taking frequent leaves of absence is less acute than in the case of a single or recently married young girl. Of

25

course, your prospective employer may know all these considerations, but you must make him aware of them at the time you apply for a job. Perhaps you can't talk him into hiring you, but you must at least try.

Create a new and interesting job opportunity for yourself if you reject run-of-the-mill employment. You may be seventy, eighty, or ninety years old, but people will still be glad to take advantage of a vocational service that is different and unique. A friend of mine who could not continue her acting career because of her age resolved her retirement problem by offering courses to housewives on preparing and serving foreign dishes. The idea was so novel that it had immediate appeal. A man I know who has traveled widely in Europe, and is now a retired teacher, supplements his school pension by advising students and their parents about prep schools and summer courses in European countries. I might mention as another example the man who had been a candlemaker in a factory, and who used his retirement to create unusual handmade candles that were individually engraved and specially designed for birthdays, weddings, and anniversaries.

Naturally, to think up such job opportunities takes much imagination and thought. However, if you are not afraid to *stretch* your imagination and to do some hard thinking and soul-searching, you may hit upon an idea that will create an unusual job ideal for you. Though we live in an age of automation, people are nevertheless willing to recognize and to pay for vocational services that are unique.

It is, of course, possible that financial circumstances and your own individual inclinations enable you to lead a life of retirement without the necessity of working. Even in such a case it is important for you to plan your day in a way that gives you a sense of accomplishment and achievement or you will begin to feel empty and purposeless. Our biological makeup makes it difficult for us to feel happy and fulfilled unless we engage in some kind of meaningful activity or have some goal and purpose.

Whether the answer to your retirement problem is all work, all play, or a little of each, you can see from the above examples that retirement does not need to be a period of retreat but can encompass active involvement and expansion. In the end, you may almost wish you had been retired all your life. You will find that you never really retire from life as long as you don't adopt *an attitude of retirement.*

CHAPTER 4

Loss of Meaning in Life

Loss of meaning in life can occur in many ways. Here are two cases which represent common aspects of this problem.

Dan, a bachelor in his fifties, came to the United States about twenty years ago from his native France. At first he struggled hard to get himself established occupationally, and his desire to make something of himself gave his life meaning and purpose. Because he was highly skilled mechanically and quite intelligent as well, he eventually managed to make a good living. As he grew older, however, a pervasive feeling of emptiness began to take hold of him. He had reached his goals, but now he did not quite know what to do with himself.

He joined several local social clubs but always felt that he did not belong because of his foreign background. Among other things, he thought that his jokes were not appreciated, and the jokes of his fellow club members did not seem funny to him. When he sought companionship in clubs that were composed of former immigrants like himself, he also felt like a stranger, thinking most members of these organizations to be either too old, too young, or too provincial. In these clubs he met several women, but found that he was afraid to be interested in those who wanted to become serious with him. On the other hand, his shyness prevented him from approaching women who appealed to him. On his job he tried to establish friend- ships, but again found that he had little in common with his co-workers. Pretty soon he gave up searching for friendship, love, or companionship. He fed himself well, dressed well, and, not having anything better to do, spent much of his spare time relaxing or sleeping. And the more he slept, the more tired he became. His clinging sense of idleness and lack of emotional satisfaction made him so cranky and irritable that he became aware of his need for therapeutic treatment.

There are quite a few "Dans" who consult psychologists with the hope that psychotherapy will help them to find new meaning and purpose in their lives. Others turn to ministers, priests, and rabbis for help. The lives of such people are like electric batteries that have been exhausted and need to be re- charged. But feelings that life is empty and meaningless are not necessarily symptoms of middle or old age. They can seize very young people too, although young people may cope with such situations in a different way.

Jackie was a young girl who had run away from home. Feelings of emptiness first appeared while she was still living with her parents. Coming home every after- noon from school, being asked the same old questions, watching the same TV programs, and going through a routine of family life where she could predict practically everything that would happen from day to day, bored her unbearably.

Finally, she became so fed up with this kind of exist- ence that she left home, got a job as a waitress, and lived by herself in New York City's Greenwich Village. She

29

thought that just living in what she fancied to be an exciting neighborhood would give her life more meaning and purpose, would make her feel more "alive." For a while, she found excitement by attending wild parties and associating with a group that was constantly moving around and "doing things." However, after the novelty of her new way of life wore off, the same feelings of emotional emptiness that she had experienced at home returned. "Doctor," she complained to me, "there is really *nothing* that can excite me. I've had it, I guess. I've tried dope, sex and liquor. I've involved myself in *avant garde* causes. It all leaves me cold and indifferent. Maybe psychotherapy will be a kick."

While Dan took a resigned attitude toward his life, Jackie tried to fight her emptiness in a more active way, hoping that diversion and "kicks" would relieve it. Both of them, however, suffered from the same sense of inner vacancy.

A *temporary* feeling of emptiness is, of course, very common. It arises most frequently when our expectations have been frustrated or when we lose a person who has previously given meaning and purpose to our lives. In the majority of instances, however, such feelings are transitory. After we have felt emotionally "washed out" for a time, life closes in over those empty places in our existences like the waves of an ocean tide flooding a beach that was barren and dry only moments before.

At other times, however, such an empty feeling may stay with us for a long period. It becomes solid and lasting like the hard lining in the blood vessels of an elderly person where arteriosclerosis prevents the free and spontaneous flow of blood. When you experience life as being empty, meaningless, and hopeless, you may almost wish yourself able to suffer pain, for *any* emotion would be better than feeling nothing at all.

How can you help yourself when a sense of emptiness and

futility overpowers you and takes the deeper meaning and purpose out of your life? Your first impulse may be to do something
drastic, risky, or exhilarating to make yourself feel more alive
and responsive. It is sometimes because of such inner emptiness
that people become involved in crime. Though they know that
the consequences of their actions could be disastrous to themselves and others, they do not care as long as they have something to relieve their emptiness and to provide them with excitement, as long as they experience a "kick" of some kind.

If your conscience and upbringing keeps you from offending the law, your sense of inner void may lead you to be belligerent, to drink too heavily, or to seek excessive and exaggerated
stimulation wherever you can find it. Should this be the case,
you will discover that the kind of excitement which is merely
created to relieve boredom and emptiness wears itself out and
only leaves you with a greater feeling of frustration and despair.
What should you do?

Change yourself and your goals. A better way of filling
your life with meaning and emotional significance would be to
change yourself, rather than your environment and external
events. The world around you is as meaningful and lively as you
make it. If you take little interest in what goes on around you,
everything will be uninteresting and dull. Naturally, just sharp-
ening your senses of observation and becoming more alert will
not relieve your sense of emptiness completely. But remember:
any small events that are experienced in a more meaningful way
will ultimately add up to a more meaningful life.

Don't be like the amateur actor who recites lines without
experiencing the emotional meaning that they convey. Instead,
try to play your role in life like a person who knows that his part
is vital, no mater how small it may be, and who communicates
this importance with serious and genuine conviction.

The sense of emptiness that you experience now may be
due to the fact that you have lost much of your own identity.

Psychologists would say that you have become *self-aliented*—a stranger to yourself. Examine the most recent years of your life and ask yourself questions like these: How many times have I expressed what I *really* thought and felt? How often have I merely pretended feelings that were not really there or my own?

It is true, of course, that custom and convention always force us to mask our real feelings to some extent. However, the habit of pretending can become so automatic and so firmly lodged within us that it carries over into too many other areas of our lives where we could afford to be more forthright and honest.

How can you drop old habits of pretending alien feelings, and become a more "real" person? For a while, try to do and to say only those things that you really believe in. For instance, don't be afraid to admit your ignorance or lack of knowledge in some fields. Admit that you are not familiar with some books that others think you should have read. Or, if you can't afford to buy certain luxuries that others can have, be frank about your situation. More important than this, don't pretend friendly or warm feelings when your genuine reaction is one of indifference or resentment. Once you become accustomed to being true to your own feelings and not dissimulating in small and in significant situations, you will be surprised how much easier it will be to act this way on those occasions which are really important to you. As you begin to be more true and genuine in your feelings and actions, you may also find that you cannot please everybody and you may meet with disapproval. However, the friendships that you do establish and the approval that you earn from others will be more honest and lasting. To lead a life that involves some pain and disappointment along with pleasure and satisfaction will give you more happiness in the long run than one which is emotionally empty and devoid of real meaning.

Thus, one way of finding more significance in life is to try to be more "yourself" than you have been in the past. However, accomplishing a change in yourself and your attitudes on your own is difficult. Someone who serves as an example of a fulfilled and emotionally rich life can help you to find yourself.

Though there are many outstanding men and women who lead or have led fulfilled, meaningful lives, I have chosen Albert Schweitzer as an example because his biography demonstrates a particularly large number of the principles and ideas which may enable you to overcome your present sense of vacuum.

Albert Schweitzer started out as a musician and writer and became famous in these careers. Then, at the age of thirty, he began to study medicine and obtained a medical degree. Not satisfied with the ordinary rewards of his profession, he left for Africa where he founded a medical mission which he has directed ever since. What are some of the characteristics that made him outstanding and led him to such a full life?

First, he had a *strong desire to be creative*. Of course, not everybody has the talent to become a creative artist, writer, or musician as Albert Schweitzer did. However, creativity is not confined to the so-called creative professions. You can be creative in the unique way that you express your love for someone, in the novel manner in which you conduct a friendship, in the style in which you live. Broadly defined, to be creative means to do something in an unusual way that generates new and strong feelings in others. Creativity of any kind can relieve feelings of emptiness.

Second, throughout his life, Schweitzer has always been filled with tremendous *intellectual curiosity and inquisitiveness*. Unfulfilled by the accomplishments of a musical career, he went on to study in the fields of science and medicine. It is almost impossible to conceive of your life as empty and meaningless when it is characterized by inquisitiveness and the desire to find out *why* things happen.

Third, an examination of Schweitzer's life demonstrates

that *he was willing to establish new and different goals* after he had reached and exhausted previous ones. He could have been content with remaining a renowned musician. As an established physician he could have been satisfied with the life of a practitioner in his own country. However, he did *not* and it kept him from falling into any kind of boring, routine existence. The blankness of many people's lives lies in the fact that they bask in an already established goal, and they do not have the initiative to go beyond such a goal, even after the old one has been reached.

Fourth, the fact that Schweitzer was willing to embark on a medical service career in a strange country shows the *courage of taking an unusual risk.* Many people suffer under the emptiness and purposelessness of their existence because excess need for security and fear of change have strangled their spirit of enterprise and their courage to take risks.

Finally, when we read Schweitzer's biography we are impressed by his *strong capacity for emotional commitment to ideals.* By emotional commitment I mean the courage to become genuinely and strongly involved with another person, group, or important cause or ideal. If you can overcome the fear of emotional commitment by learning to identify with something that transcends the boundaries of your own self-interest, you will feel that your life can never be completely empty or meaningless.

Try to relieve emptiness by establishing more meaningful relationships with others. There is no better and more effective way to relieve a sense of emptiness than to find a new and emotionally satisfying relationship. Perhaps it is the only real way in which a shallow and empty period in life can be ended. What can compare to the sense of exhilaration that we experience after we have established a promising friendship or after we have found someone whose love for us makes us look at our own lives in a different way? For the individual who has lived in a state of psychological hibernation, it is like the appearance of spring after a long, cold winter.

It is therefore not surprising that many people who complain about the emptiness and meaninglessness of their lives make statements like these: "If I could only meet someone for whom I really cared, everything would be so different. It would be like a miracle." Unfortunately, miracles do not happen very often, and our search for people who will mean something to us is often long and frustrating.

Are there any ways and means which could facilitate the finding of "real," meaningful people in your life? Are there any errors that you should avoid? Let me give you some pointers.

My first suggestion: *You yourself must have faith and confidence in your ability to find people who can enhance the meaning of your life.* Of course, this may not happen today, tomorrow, or even next month, but you must be convinced that it will happen *some* time. It is your confidence and your positive attitude of accepting other people that will draw others more closely to you.

Go out of your way to meet as many people as you can in order to better your chances for finding the one person who will really matter to you. This may even mean, on occasion, having the courage to meet people to whom you have not been introduced formally. You can sometimes meet the most fascinating and *worthwhile* people at strange places and under odd circumstances, but you won't if you narrow your social range of activities too much.

A mistake that is frequently made in searching for more meaningful relationships is to try to find them among people who do interesting work or lead interesting lives. However, it is not the kind of work a person performs or the social status that a person holds that counts. So-called interesting and important people can often be very boring when you get to know them

35

better. For example, a famous author may be at his best in his novels and essays, but might be a poor husband, lover, or friend. An outstanding executive may demonstrate ingenuity and aggressiveness in his business campaigns, but be weak and overly submissive in his private life.

Don't jeopardize your chances for finding an emotionally meaningful relationship because of your own hidden prejudices and personal biases. How many people say—"Mr. B. is a wonderful man. If he were only older . . . Miss S. is lovely, but how can I get along with her since she does not share the same interests I have . . . Mr. J. is a nice man but I don't like the way he dresses, and I would not like to be seen with him." People who voice such opinions ought to realize that they themselves erect walls which block potentially meaningful relationships. Though the voiced objections may be well founded, it's wise to remember that all of us are not at our best when we meet new people. It may be not incidental that the Greek word for "personality" originally meant "mask." How easy it is to mistake a social mask for the real person. When you meet someone, wipe out previous reservations and prejudices. Don't take people at face value alone, and don't let your own prejudices interfere with your first impressions. In perceiving a newly introduced person, your mind should be as clear as fresh, unused film in a camera.

Try to keep relationships which are already established from stagnating and becoming meaningless. What you do at *every* moment of a relationship will determine how meaningful and lasting it will be. The understanding way in which you respond to a loved person's temporary moods will sometimes be more essential than fancy promises for the future and lengthy oaths of loving allegiance. How vividly you react to a story or a joke that is told to you by the person whom you like may communicate a greater feeling of concern than the gifts you might buy or the sacrifices you make. Only by fully experiencing every second of a relationship with sensitivity to its most subtle nuances and demands can the meaningfulness of an emotional tie be retained over a long period of time. The deeper meaning of many marriage and love relationships too often gets lost not because of a lack of common goals, but because of deficient responsiveness to what was wished for at a particular time and moment. Sometimes the care with which a husband wraps a blanket around his wife may mean more to her than his ardent sexual advances. In short, a relationship that *continues* to be meaningful is always the result of many past meaningful moments.

A relationship becomes empty and shallow only if it becomes *void of ideals and high expectations.* Love or friendship comes to a dead end once you accept either one as a finished product that can no longer be changed.

Don't let petty arguments, temporary irritations, and disappointments destroy the image that you have previously formed of the person who has come to mean so much to you. Perhaps the person you like is not always as attentive, understanding, resourceful, strong, and alert as you were once led to believe. How easy it is, then, to become discouraged and disillusioned. But if you continue to *believe in,* and *express belief in,* those character qualities that you previously perceived in the other person, your faith may bring them back to reality. People tend to want to live up to another's high opinion of them. History abounds with examples of men and women who developed their finest personality traits because of the faith that others had in their potential capacities, even though those qualities were not *always* apparent.

Another reason why relationships between two people sometimes stagnate is because *certain phases of the relationship have been overemphasized* to the exclusion of others. A friendship becomes dull and empty if it consists primarily of intellectual discussion and lacks the sharing of other interests and experiences. Even sexual activities can lose some of their thrill if they form the *only* basis of a love relationship. Holding hands in dim candlelight and drinking Chianti cease to add a romantic glow if such activities become habit patterns. To inject new life into a relationship that is beginning to fade would therefore require changing those activities that have been overly indulged in to others that are new.

It is important to mention in this connection, too, that the meaningfulness of a relationship does not always grow with a great deal of closeness and the sharing of all experiences. There are many individuals who share every trouble and joy together and yet remain emotional strangers at heart. *Excessive* familiarity in daily activities cannot only breed contempt but can also lead to emptiness and indifference, the elements that kill the deeper meaning of a relationship. It is important to achieve some kind of balance between "togetherness" and "apartheid" (separateness).

The lives of two people should not be like neighboring trees which, because of their close proximity, sometimes deprive each other of sunshine and nourishment. Rather, the lives of people who are close should more appropriately be compared to the branches of neighboring trees that extend toward each other, yet do not intertwine.

A close relationship can sometimes lose its fervor and meaning *because the people involved isolate themselves too much from outside social contacts.* Regardless of how much two individuals have to offer each other and how self-sufficient they may be, they could not exist on an island *à deux* for an indefinite period of time.

A meaningful relationship can go to pieces *because basic problems and difficulties are evaded.* The sudden empty feeling that sometimes arises between two people who have been close before is often the result of seemingly trivial misunderstandings that were glossed over when they should have been clarified. Therefore, don't permit an expression of disappointment or a slightly angry silence to fester until it has grown to such significant proportions that it creates an unbridgeable distance between yourself and another. Talk out your problems with one another without recriminations.

Realize that it is natural for every close and continuous association to contain some moments of emptiness and even boredom. It is only with people whom we meet on a less intimate basis that we can avoid some of the drudgery of everyday living, and even then this is not always possible. Therefore, do not lose faith in an otherwise sound and meaningful relationship if it seems void and empty on occasions. If there were no emotionally empty periods in our lives, we would not be able to appreciate the times that are filled with a sense of fulfillment and satisfaction.

CHAPTER 5 / Suicidal
Thoughts

The following cases illustrate the widely divergent pressures
that can bring a human being to the tragic decision for suicide.

A phone call late at night: "Doctor, I hope I'm not
disturbing you at this late hour, but I just had to call you.
I want to tell you not to worry any more. Im going to be
all right. You know, I'm going to be the best patient youve
ever had. Have I been drinking? Of course not. Is that
your first association, doctor? Ha-ha—well, goodbye now
—and sorry to disturb you. I won't do it again—ever."

The phone call came from Liz E., a patient of mine
who had never before called me outside of my regular
office hours. Liz E. was a widow. Her husband had died a
few months earlier. She had been a singer and possessed
many of the traits that are commonly associated with
artists: great impatience, dead-serious devotion to work,
and an impulsive, explosive temperament that flared up
at the slightest provocation. Whenever I said things that
touched a sensitive nerve in her defensive personality, she
used to throw matchbooks at me. Once she hurled a letter
opener at me as I sat behind my desk. I had suggested to
her that a period of hospitalization might be advisable for
her and she had shouted, "Doctor, I'd rather kill myself
than do that!" The word "kill" occurred frequently in her
vocabulary. When she consulted me at first she firmly

denied the presence of any suicidal ideas. "Suicide?" She shrugged her shoulders. "Why should I do that? What do you think I am, a nut?"

Liz's reaction to her husband's death was externally calm and detached. She refused to see me for a long time after it happened. So when she called me that night I became upset about her reasons for getting in touch with me. Though she did not seem to be a depressed patient, her impulsiveness had often made me consider the possibility that she might commit suicide. Therefore I did not hesitate to rush to her side after I had received the call. My suspicion was not unfounded; she had taken an overdose of pills, but fortunately it was possible to get her to a hospital in time, and her life was saved.

* * *

Bob, the son of a prominent physician, was an 18-year-old college student. Although he was never very successful in high school, he was admitted to an Ivy League college—the same that his father had attended. During his first term at college everything went well. He conscientiously followed the study schedule that had been mapped out for him by his college adviser. Suddenly his marks began to drop and despite intensive study he was unable to keep up with his class work. He seriously began to doubt his academic abilities, and it became more and more difficult for him to keep his mind on the complicated textbooks. He succumbed to the lure of daydreams. Feelings of inadequacy about his chances of getting admitted to medical school and becoming a doctor like his famous father began to creep up. At about this time he met a young lady who was considered one of the most popular and attractive girls on the campus, and she gave Bob her almost undivided attention. He began to cut classes in order to see her and he found that studying made his vision become blurred and fuzzy.

A shy and overly serious boy during his adolescence, he had never been very successful with girls. Though even now he felt somewhat anxious in the presence of the girl he loved, her attention to him seemed to enhance his self-confidence. However, Bob's confidence faltered rapidly when the girl developed a crush on another student. She pursued this young man with the same intensity with which she had previously overwhelmed Bob. To make matters worse, Bob discovered just about this time that he had not been accepted by one of the fraternities which had rushed him. Suddenly he felt defeated on all fronts of his life. *Having no previous experiences of success and achievement to fall back on,* he felt that he would be a failure in everything all of his life. His unsuccessful past seemed to be the only standard he could use to judge what was in store for him in the future.

One morning he was found dead outside the dormitory. He had killed himself by jumping from a fifth-floor window.

❋   ❋   ❋

Joan had been married to Mike for five years. She had met her husband at the young people's group of a church, and he had impressed her immediately as an unusually stable and mature person. At last, she felt, she had met a man whom she could really *respect.* Her idealized image of him remained untouched during the first year of their marriage. Then, however, things changed. The image turned out to be false. Mike became extremely critical of whatever she did: of the way she dressed, of her friends and her family, and of the way she prepared food. A violent temper that apparently had been held in check emerged in Mike's character. Where there had been tenderness and consideration before, there was now nothing but impatience and criticism.

At first Joan blamed everything on circumstances. Perhaps, she thought, it was only one of those crises that people are supposed to go through during the first years of marital adjustment. "You must wait and be patient," she said to herself. But one year, two years, five years passed and nothing changed. Gradually she began to realize that Mike's temperamental and egocentric personality was real. What she had fallen in love with had been merely a façade, a role which he had used to cover up his true self.

As the problems, arguments, and flare-ups repeated themselves with a regularity that seemed unbearable, Joan became convinced that their marriage would probably always be this way. But her religious convictions made it impossible for her to consider divorce. Her life, which she had centered around her marriage, lost all its meaning.

When Mike returned from work one evening he found his home filled with gas fumes and his wife dead by the stove.

In reading about these and other cases of suicide it is often easy to understand some of the circumstances that led up to them, but more difficult to explain the deeper and perhaps more essential psychological factors at the core of such tragedies.

We may then ask ourselves some of the following questions: What are the circumstances which cause some fifteen to twenty thousand individuals to choose suicide every year? Are there some who are more "suicide-prone" than others? Are people who commit the act of suicide temporarily robbed of their sanity when they try it? What, if anything, can be done to prevent suicide? And are there some warning signals that may enable us to take precautionary measures before it is too late?

Perhaps the complete answers to such questions may never

43

be known. However, some understanding has been gained from the research conducted by hospitals and clinics that have cared for attempted suicides. And some knowledge has been derived from the notes that have been left by those successful in killing themselves. Let me give you the essence of this research.

PSYCHOLOGICAL AND SOCIOLOGICAL FACTORS

Glorification of Death Most of us have very definite notions and concepts about death, and because we do not like to think at length about them, it is natural for us to repress them most of our lives. They determine our unconscious attitudes toward suicide.

Some people think about death as something peaceful and soothing, like the healthful sleep that sometimes follows sickness and results in recovery. The notion of rebirth after death is closely connected with such ideas.

The desirability of death may be similarly enhanced by the concept that it can be something which relieves us of our feelings of guilt about bad deeds which we have performed.

It has been found that some individuals who commit suicide have looked at death as something that is positive rather than negative. Perhaps such an attitude made them more prone to seek this way out of difficulties than those people who look at death as something that is final, horrible, and completely destructive.

Geography and Religion Differences in the suicide rate among various nations has given rise to the notion that geographical and sociological factors play a significant role. There is some statistical evidence that more people in Scandinavian countries commit suicide than those living in the more sunny and warm Mediterranean regions. However, in view of the complex and highly individual reasons that cause suicide, it would seem too quick a generalization to attribute it to climate or social structure. (We have no reliable accounts on the exact suicide rate in Communist-oriented nations.)

It is likely that religious attitudes exert a more definite influence on the occurrence of suicide. It is considered a sin to kill oneself in the Catholic religion, but is looked upon somewhat more tolerantly by the followers of the Protestant faith. Therefore, it stands to reason that devout Catholics are sometimes less prone to suicidal self-destruction than are Protestants.

Mental Illness Some people believe that every individual who resorts to suicide must be insane or at least temporarily insane. Whether one subscribes to this idea would depend upon one's definition of insanity. If it is viewed merely as a state of heightened emotional confusion and suggestibility under duress, this might perhaps apply. However, many psychologists and psychiatrists believe that there are degrees of mental confusion, and that the exact borderline between being "sane" or "insane" is often hard to draw. Many seriously disturbed patients who are in mental hospitals and under psychiatric care are *not* suicide-prone. On the other hand, quite a few only mildly disturbed and often quite well-adjusted persons have entertained suicidal ideas and have carried them out.

Depression Many psychiatrists believe that there is a very close connection between depression and suicide. Sigmund Freud, the founder of psychoanalysis, thought that depression involves rage that is actually intended for someone else but has become self-directed, and that suicide must be the end result of this process. Thus, it is postulated by some followers of Freudian psychology that no one commits suicide without the unconscious desire to kill someone else. I believe that this interpretation may apply to some cases of suicide, but perhaps not to all. One factor that can be adduced against this theory is that many severely depressed people often do *not* commit suicide. The depression may be the result and not the cause of manifestations of suicide.

Personality Types I don't think it makes much difference whether a person is introverted, extraverted, or ambiverted when it comes to the possibility of suicide. However, there are

45

some indications that individuals whose everyday behavior is marked by excess impulsiveness are somewhat more susceptible.

Chronological Age Suicides have been known to occur with some frequency during early and late adolescence, and during the period of menopause or the climacteric. There is, of course, no chronological age that does not have its emotional crises, and therefore suicide can occur at any period of life—if the individual is prone to take this way out of difficulties.

It may be worthwhile mentioning at this point that there is no conclusive scientific evidence that suicide is inherited, though at times it does seem to occur with more than average frequency in some families.

The Loss Of Meaning and Purpose in Life This is perhaps one of the most basic causes of suicide. Loss of meaning signifies that the suicidal individual is convinced of the complete and irrevocable futility of his life. Since life without some purpose or meaning is empty and intolerable, death is chosen as a less painful alternative. Sometimes the lack of meaning in life is felt instantly and intuitively. At other times it is a feeling that grows and finally takes root in one's mind.

A saying which has survived from ancient times is that man cannot live by bread alone. This statement conveys that just feeding oneself, or merely going through the physical motions of existing without some goal or meaning attached to it, is never enough. The person who contemplates suicide is under the impression that some of the basic reasons for living—receiving and giving love, expressing oneself, relating to others, and gaining approval and emotional satisfaction—have ceased to exist for him and he is no longer capable of anticipating them.

A brief examination of the suicidal cases described at the beginning of this chapter will demonstrate that the loss of the meaning in life was an important factor in all three cases.

In the case of Liz E., it was the death of her husband that provided the basic motivation for her suicide attempt. Bob, the college student who committed suicide, was unable to see how his life could serve any further meaningful purpose if it was going to involve the same failures and defeats; and lack of previous experience prevented him from seeing how the future could be any different. Joan, the unhappily married woman, was driven to self-destruction after her marriage had become meaningless. Unable to break it off and yet incapable of continuing it, life no longer held those goals and values that could make it worthwhile for her.

IF YOU YOURSELF ARE BOTHERED BY SUICIDAL IDEAS . . .

People who want to commit suicide and are serious about it have usually arrived at the conclusion "not to be" as the result of much thought, after considerable hesitation, and as a consequence of repeatedly painful experiences. To say to an individual who is contemplating suicide, "Don't do it. Life is more wonderful than you think," must seem like a ridiculous oversimplification of the intense mental anguish and despair that he is experiencing. If someone offered this advice to you, you would probably feel that he was trying to extinguish a fire by pouring a few glasses of water on it.

If your mind is set on suicide, not words but new experiences, a new purpose for living, or loving and being loved, are the only things than can dissuade you from taking your life. The little that is known about the psychological causes of suicide (that it is a form of internalized aggression, that it is tied up with your past attitudes toward death, that it is essentially an escape) would hardly be enough to deter you from taking the fatal step you are contemplating.

Almost every person who is contemplating suicide, however, has some doubts about it, and not all suicide attempts are impulsive. It is not uncommon to find that those who decide to take the death jump from high buildings spend hours of doubting and hesitating before taking the fatal leap. It seems that the

47

drive to live, though muted under depression and despair, can never be completely silenced.

If you are seriously contemplating suicide, let me make an appeal to those forces in you that still pull you in the direction of living.

Realize that your wish to die may be an exaggerated and distorted response to a situation of stress. Suppose sudden financial loss has made you lose interest in life. Under the influence of this blow, you *over-rate* the value of money. Your mind becomes rigidly fixed on what money can do for your life instead of seeing monetary rewards as not the only source of life's satisfactions. Or suppose a person who has given your life deep meaning is no longer with you. The feeling of utter desperation that seizes you blinds you to everything else that has emotional value. Again, you are selecting *one* aspect of your life situation and are completely ignoring and distorting others. Perhaps you feel that the process of aging and the gradual loss of strength and health are completely intolerable to you. Your extensive preoccupation with the fear of aging could become a mountain that obstructs your view of anything worthwhile.

What has been said here has been confirmed many times by therapists. Therapeutic sessions with individuals who have contemplated suicide have often shown that the patients' self-destructive drives were due to the attachment of an exaggerated significance to one aspect of living and to a rigid fixation upon it. Realize that regardless of how tragic a loss or how severe a disappointment may seem to you at a given moment, you are always over-reacting to it.

Realize that one of the fundamental principles of life is change. Many people contemplate suicide because of an almost irrational belief that the conditions which cause their distress are permanent. It is true, of course, that some of life's losses are irreplaceable, that there are illnesses which are chronic, and that nothing can restore the powers of youth to the aging individual.

But it is also true that even the most severe physical or emotional pain *undergoes some change with time* and never remains as intensely felt as at the time it is inflicted or shortly thereafter. That situations can improve is almost inconceivable to the person who is under emotional stress. The pain robs him of the capacity to visualize change for the better. If you experience emotional myopia, you should realize that you are operating under a temporary illusion, that your belief in a permanent *status quo* is basically distorted and contrary to the laws of living. You only stand still on life's road if you yourself stop.

You should not feel ashamed or hesitate to seek psychiatric help. This does not mean that you suffer from a mental disorder or that the psychiatrist whom you consult will confine you to an institution to prevent you from carrying out your suicidal plans. It could mean, however, that you are taking a first step toward reorganizing your life and learning about some of the unconscious bases of your suicidal ideas. Research that has been conducted with suicidal patients has shown that they can be helped. Even brief psychotherapy could be of assistance.

A therapist cannot always change the situations that have led you to thoughts of suicide, but he can try to change your *attitudes* toward them. A changed attitude may give you a new outlook on life

You may feel that only you yourself can understand the causes for your contemplated suicide and therefore refuse outside help. Try to see that all of us lose our sense of proportion and judgment under emotional stress. Depression, disappointment, intense frustration, and sudden loss can affect our minds just as toxins influence bodily functions. Of course, there *are* times when we can't be responsible for our own actions and don't know what is best for ourselves. But just as you should trust a physician when you have a physical ailment, you should not hesitate to seek professional help when self-destructive impulses temporarily incapacitate you.

There are places and people ready to help you if you are willing to make the effort to find them. There is an organization called the National Save-a-Life League whose headquarters are located in New York City. The New York address is 505 Fifth Avenue and the telephone number is MUrray Hill 7-2142. Branches of this organization are now in various cities throughout the United States and you can find them by referring to the local telephone directory or by communicating with the headquarters office in New York. They conduct a 24-hour phone service. Psychiatrists and social workers are on the staff of this organization.

The name of another organization of this kind is Rescue, Incorporated, and it is affiliated with the Boston City Hospital at 745 Massachusetts Avenue (telephone HAncock 6-6600). Its staff includes physicians, psychologists, psychiatrists, ministers, rabbis, social workers, and nurses.

There are two churches in Chicago which have set up a telephone service for suicidal persons. One of them is called the Peoples Church of Chicago. The telephone number is LOng Beach 1-9595. The other is the Central Church of Chicago, and its facilities are available by calling DEarborn 2-4840.

A 24-hour telephone answering service is also maintained by an organization which calls itself "Friends" and is located in Dade County, Florida. The telephone number is FRanklin 4-3637 and it spells out the word "friends" on the dial. The purpose of this organization is to provide employment, medical, psychiatric, or religious help as needed.

There is a suicide prevention center which is located on the grounds of the Los Angeles County General Hospital (P. O. Box 3398, Los Angeles 31, California).

HOW TO HELP OTHERS WHO HAVE CONTEMPLATED OR HAVE TRIED TO COMMIT SUICIDE

Crucial life situations that could provoke suicidal thoughts

and ideas are (1) periods of depression which manifest themselves indirectly by a generalized loss of interest, inability to
concentrate, refusal to eat, over-all inertia and apathy in everyday living; (2) sudden loss of a person through death; (3) after
severe and often seemingly incurable physical illness or incapacity; (4) after disappointment in connection with a love
relationship; (5) after unwanted pregnancy; (6) after the menopause for women or climacteric for men; and (7) after severe
financial reverses or the loss of previous source of income and
livelihood. Many studies on suicide prevention have shown that
the experience of *loss* of any kind is a most crucial condition. The
suicide-prone person, therefore, needs special care and attention
when crises of this kind overwhelm him.

The most important measure in trying to keep a person
from committing suicide is to provide him with *distraction*
which should precede dissuasion.

Since most cases of suicide are caused by emotional rather
than rational considerations, attempts to prevent it by the use of
logical arguments may be as difficult as convincing an individual
who is in love that he is not. Distraction often means listening
over and over again to the suicidal person's woes and troubles
if he or she is willing to talk about them. Distraction could also
mean removing the individual (if possible) from the environment in which the suicide was attempted, or making him talk
about or discuss different things.

The discovery of an attempted suicide is no time to engage
the suicidal individual in long arguments about *why* he tried it,
or to make promises that often cannot be fulfilled later. (I'll
never leave you again. I'll marry you. You can have anything
you want.) Perhaps the best attitude is one of warm and genuine
care. If too much fuss is made, the person involved will only
feel *more* guilty about what he has done. From a long range
point of view the best measure to prevent recurrence would be
some form of psychotherapy. This may be psychoanalysis or

51

some other form of continuous professional counseling.

If professional help is not available or the individual involved resists it strongly, friends and relatives must try to do the best they can under the circumstances. They can be most helpful not by what they *say* to the suicidal person but by what they *do* for him. This means being available (whenever possible) when help is sought, spending much time with the afflicted individual, doing things that he likes, and keeping him active and occupied.

In trying to prevent future suicide attempts, an attitude of overwatchfulness may be resented by the person involved because he may think he is being robbed of his freedom and treated like a child who is constantly observed by his parents.

If an individual decides against suicide, it should ideally be something that has come from himself. Too much of an attempt to influence the suicidal person may only strengthen a desire to stick to his own point of view that life is worthless.

That a person says he has given up his suicidal ideas or is more cheerful in mood and attitude is, of course, no indication that the danger of suicide is over. He may merely act compliant and less concerned because he is no longer in conflict about the issue and has resigned himself to making another and more successful attempt to kill himself. Continued concern on the part of those who are worried about the suicidal person is therefore necessary.

The best cure for the person who is addicted to self-destruction is for him to see more meaning and significance in his life, for him to have some worthwhile goals. Any method that can be used to achieve these would be justified.

CAUSES FOR DEPRESSIONS

I have chosen the following cases to demonstrate some of the underlying and often unconscious reasons for depression.

> When Hank got into one of his depressed moods he would be extremely irritable for several days, would barely speak, or only do so in a subdued voice, and could not concentrate on his work.
>
> Hank was particularly disturbed about his depressions because they interfered with what he loved most—teaching children. Perhaps he had chosen the teaching field because he needed others to look up to him, and he needed to be put into a role of authority. In any event, I found in my interview with Hank that his private life was essentially empty. He rarely participated in social events. Although he was in his late thirties, he had been unable to become genuinely interested in women, and he said that he had never fallen in love.
>
> What caused Hank's depressions? His loneliness? A sense of frustration derived from his feeling of inadequacy? These reasons seemed too superficial an explanation.
>
> Two factors finally provided a clue to the basic

reasons for his depression. One was that Hank's depression occurred exclusively at times when he was with his pupils in school. They never occurred when he was at home. The second clue was derived from Hank's dreams, which he reported to me during treatment. Almost all these dreams centered around men or boys, and the dreams were marked by terror and anxiety.

Finally Hank confessed to me that on occasion he felt unusually attracted to the boys whom he taught, and that he did not know what to do about it.

In the course of psychological treatment it became clear that his depressions represented a form of self-punishment for his forbidden wishes. His *fear* of having homosexual inclinations bothered him most. With the help of therapy he eventually learned to handle such fears with less anxiety. He began to take a more active interest in his social life, and started to date more frequently. As he felt less guilty, his depressions disappeared.

That depressions sometimes express self-love and self-indulgence rather than self-punishment is demonstrated by the following case.

Mrs. D. complained that she had been almost continually depressed for the last *ten* years! She attributed her pervasive melancholy to the sudden death of her daughter Sheila, who at the age of twelve had been the victim of a cerebral hemorrhage. Closer scrutiny of Mrs. D.'s childhood revealed that she had grown up in an overprotective environment, and had been very much spoiled by her parents. I got the impression that Mrs. D. had been prone to moodiness practically all her life, and that this moodiness had been indirectly strengthened by her parents. As a child, she had frequently resorted to tears or sulks to make her parents yield to her wishes.

Mrs. D.'s marriage had been an unhappy one, and although her husband was kind and understanding she had little genuine respect for him. She had hoped that having a child would cement their relationship, and it did for a little while.

However, after the young girl's unexpected death Mrs. D.'s buried feelings against her husband came to the surface again. Though she did not argue with her husband, she assumed a very cold and distant attitude toward him, rationalizing this attitude by attributing it to the death of her daughter. She became as sullen, moody, and withdrawn as she had been in her childhood. She continually wallowed in her grief, and withdrew from almost all social relationships during her period of mourning. Her husband tried to divert her attention by taking her on trips. He gave her expensive and carefully chosen gifts. However, nothing could please Mrs. D. and she began more and more to give in to her moodiness.

Although Mrs. D. had consulted many psychiatrists she held on to her depression with a tenacity that defied all attempts at change. Subconsciously she *wanted* to be depressed, as this allowed her to maneuver her husband and others in the same way as she had manipulated her parents as a child.

*　　*　　*

Nina was a woman in her fifties who consulted me because of depressions connected with what might be called a weekend neurosis. Whenever a weekend approached, a feeling of gloom and despair would overcome her. It resulted in crying spells which she tried to relieve by taking tranquilizers. When these did not seem to work, she would resort to heavy drinking which only plunged her into deeper feelings of hopelessness and depression.

Nina's previous life had been difficult in several respects. She had lost both of her parents at an early age, and had been brought up by her grandparents, whose only interest was to make her economically self-supporting at the earliest opportunity.

Bored with the usual sales job, Nina obtained employment as a taxi-girl in one of the dance halls in her neighborhood. The contacts which she made with her male customers led her gradually but persistently in the direction of prostitution. Later, her call-girl activities enabled her to go to resorts and places of entertainment that she had always wished to visit as an adolescent. Although she occasionally felt anxious when she became aware of some of the dangers of her newly chosen profession, essentially she took the life of a prostitute in her stride, and had little if any desire to settle down and get married.

When Nina came to me as a patient, she had come to the end of her career as a call-girl. She had lost much of her youthful appeal, her health had begun to falter, and she no longer earned the large amounts of money that she had in her youth. Although she managed to get a job as a bookkeeper, it only gave her a small income and little personal satisfaction.

Her dire circumstances would, of course, be enough to depress anyone. However, it was not really her low-income situation or the loss of her appeal that bothered her so deeply, for Nina was accustomed to living an unstable and unpredictable life. What she really lacked was any sense of purpose, direction, or goal in her life. She could not see herself in the role of a wife or mother. (Her age precluded the prospect of having children.) By the same token, something within herself said a sharp and definite *no* when she thought of resuming her former call-girl activities. Not knowing what to do with her life, having no past to go back to and no future in sight, she felt deeply frustrated. The lack of any purpose and goal in her life accumulated in her like a poison, spreading slowly, and then hitting her suddenly in the form of depression. This depression was actually not caused by any definite loss or misfortune, but represented a general feeling of hopelessness and resignation.

It took a long time for Nina to get her feet on the ground again. Finally she managed to get a job which held her interest in a travel bureau. She met a man who was willing to accept her on her own merits and was also willing to overlook her shady past. When this happened, her depressions became less frequent and ultimately disappeared altogether.

The kind of depressive moods that you yourself experience may not be as severe and as damaging as those which I have tried to portray here. Nevertheless, I think that even light and more transitory states of moodiness and depression are sometimes due to the same psychological causes which characterize those I have described.

It is true, of course, that there are many states of depression that cannot be explained on a purely psychological basis. The weather, our blood chemistry, physical injuries and pains, fatigue or overwork, and myriads of other causes can affect our moods profoundly. However, without denying the importance of all these factors, our own attitudes and the subjective intensity with which we react to these external influences often make the difference between a more severe depression and one that is tolerable and can be overcome.

METHODS OF FIGHTING DEPRESSION

Seek active self-expression. When you feel depressed, your desire is to withdraw into apathy and passivity. If you are willing to fight this trend, you will be on your way to recovery.

"Action dispels fear" is an old saying which can also be made to apply to states of depression. Activity of a physical kind may help. Go out and take a walk if you can. A depressed patient once told me that he found it helpful to do knee-bends and push-ups when "the blues" tried to get the upper hand in his life. Swimming, boating, tennis, bowling, or similar activities have helped many temporarily depressed people.

If you can't or don't want to engage in physical activities, try to do something else that permits you to express your feelings. *Force yourself* to become absorbed in some form of self-expression. Play the piano, write a letter, repair a tool or gadget, clean your desk or your apartment! *Do something!* No matter what it is, you will feel better than if you remain passive.

Avoid objects and places that carry a sentimental meaning while you are in a state of depression. If you feel depressed because of the loss of a loved one, you must try to eliminate all stimuli that bring him or her to mind.

Gifts that were received from the loved person should be put out of sight. Avoid streets and places that you visited with your lover if this is at all possible. Don't listen to the radio programs or special records that you used to enjoy together. Don't go to movies where the main plot centers around love. Don't read fiction or poetry that has a sentimental appeal. Naturally, it is impossible *never* to think of the person you love. You can't eliminate painful thoughts, but you can avoid some of the stimuli and associations that may provoke them.

Anticipate the times when you are most prone to depression and plan some distraction for them. Though depressions may come unexpectedly, they sometimes occur more frequently during certain days and hours. Some people feel blue during the morning, others during the evening and still others at night. A large number of individuals get depressed when the weekend comes around. I used to know a young man whose depressions were caused by beautiful weather, because it made him more sadly aware of his own dark and gloomy feelings. A patient of mine who is divorced had a regular depressive spell at four o'clock, the time when his children (they were in his ex-wife's custody) used to come home from school.

Thus, the particular time when your depression occurs can provide a clue as to what causes it. Too, beforehand knowledge of when you will be depressed may make it possible for you to take preventive action. Perhaps you can arrange not to be left alone during your periods of despondency. Or you could plan ahead to be busy with some work that distracts you and demands your undivided attention.

Don't associate with people who make you feel more depressed. In trying to socialize, you may seek the company of people who, without intending to, make your mood worse than it was before. This may be particularly true if you associate with individuals who are in many ways better off than yourself. For instance, if you are a lonely bachelor, visiting a recently married and very happy couple when you are depressed could obviously make you more depressed.

Don't be a martyr. Perhaps nobody is more prey to the "martyr complex" than the person who is under the influence of a prolonged depression. To succumb to a martyr complex means that you add a special touch of glamor and glory to your present misery. This may, of course, be one way of relieving the feelings of melancholy from which you suffer. However, while playing the martyr role may help you temporarily, it can actually *prolong* your agony: you may get so accustomed to this frame of mind that you find it hard to abandon. Besides, a chronic self-appointed martyr, though pitied and sympathized with, is rarely liked.

On the basis of past experience, find your own way of relieving depression. The particular way in which you can change a mood that upsets you is, of course, a highly subjective matter. Your best guides in knowing how *you* can overcome gloomy moods is your own past experience and some knowledge of yourself.

You may have found that you must be left alone when things bother you, and that talking with others only makes you feel worse. In that case, follow your own intuition, and don't let anybody drag you into social participation. Withdrawal can be a good adjustment technique at times, provided it is temporary and not carried to an extreme. An occasional retreat from everything can sometimes cleanse your psychological system of any emotional poisons that have accumulated. It is like going on a diet after you have eaten too much.

If, on the other hand, your past experience has taught you that your feelings of gloom are relieved most effectively by losing yourself in a wild round of social activities, you may need to get away from yourself in order to get back to yourself! If this is the case, once again it is wise to follow your natural inclinations.

You may be the kind of person who is helped in getting over a depressive mood through the solace and relief of communicating with nature.

Make sure that whatever you do when a depression syndrome occurs, it is consistent with your personality and your style of living.

CHAPTER 7

First Aid for Addicts
Overeating,
Overdrinking, Oversmoking

Every year books are printed that tell you how to get slim with-out really trying, how to lose weight by using self-hypnosis, how to diagnose your own form of dypsomania, or how to hate cig-arettes. It all sounds so easy in the books. The authors assure you that *they* have tried it, and that they *easily* abandoned old established habits. Where case histories are used, they always illustrate that as soon as a patient learns a given technique, he will be cured immediately. I often think how many authors of books on weight reduction would starve if they could not sell lit-erature to people who don't know how to starve themselves!

Many of these promising self-help books turn out to be disappointing after you have purchased them. Though you could probably get a refund "if not 100% satisfied," by the time you have finished reading you are too tired of it all to bother.

If you expect this chapter to offer quick new remedies or gimmicks on how to get rid of such oral addictions as over-smoking, overdrinking or overeating, you will be disappointed. Instead, I would like to tell you how some of my patients have tried to overcome addictions to food and alcohol. If you have similar problems, you may be able to benefit from their experi-ence.

When I saw the first patient (I shall call him Bert to disguise his identity), I recognized him immediately. I had often seen his obese body on television. He was a well-known comedian. Though he worried about his corpulence, it was his very chubbiness which was partly responsible for his success in show business. I noticed that he carried a large bag with him. As I interviewed him, I was surprised to see that this bag contained hero sandwiches, which he eagerly began to munch while describing his emotional difficulties.

As in the case of many individuals of this kind, Bert's obesity dated back to childhood. Though Bert did not distinguish himself academically in school, he was the most husky child in his class, and this gave him a certain amount of attention, but of course not the kind he wanted. His present problem was, however, that he had had a heart attack which was linked to his obesity. It had become an essential matter of health for him to take off weight. Yet he was unable to eliminate from his diet the pies and candies that had become almost as important to him as the salary he received for his TV appearances. Previously, he had been analyzed, hypnotized, and had also spent time on "health farms." Whenever he lost a little weight he regained it rapidly. The problem was: how could he be helped?

✿   ✿   ✿

Isabelle, the second patient whom I shall describe, was originally an extremely slim young girl. She worked as a receptionist in a reducing salon and had been hired as a living example of the efficacy of the courses. That she was slender had not been the result of courses, but of previous poverty and undernourishment. Isabelle worked in the reducing salon for several years, and even as she grew older her employers were pleased to notice that "middle-age spread" did not set in. However, suddenly, and seemingly without detectable medical cause, Isabelle began to take a tremendous interest in eating, and consumed king-size portions wherever she went. Soon she began to put on those excess pounds which her place of employment was in business to take off. It was at this point that Isabelle consulted me, since the salon had threatened to fire her.

Both patients—Bert and Isabelle—came to me in what was to them an acute state of emergency. Both had read books on dieting and had been to medical specialists, but something always seemed to keep them from following through on the suggestions that were made to them. Psychologists would say that they were both poorly motivated. Psychoanalysts would state that they had an unconscious need to become fat, or to remain so. Perhaps it was all due to improper feeding as infants (bottle frustration). In fact, that is exactly what Bert had been told by one of the analysts whom he had consulted. However, this insight did not help him one bit. Though he believed he had clarified the causes of his problem, this knowledge did not reduce his hunger at all. Isabelle, too, had been told that she was starved for love as an infant, and that she tried to make up for it by overeating. Or that she resented her poverty-filled childhood, and was now rebelling against the "idle rich" who had everything she had been denied.

How could I help these patients? Their dilemma was my problem. In an attempt to solve it, I studied psychological and psychoanalytical literature on the causes of obesity. I learned to my amazement that even the classical Greeks had experimented with a magic potion which was meant to keep a person always slim, and that some African mothers practiced the curious custom of fattening up their daughters to be more eligible for marriage. I also read a great deal on oral fixation, aggression, and frustration. But how could this aid me in my treatment of Bert and Isabelle? What was the practical solution?

It was in connection with a third patient that one of the basic elements for the cure of addictions and habits became clear to me.

Leila K.'s original home was Iran and she had come to live in the United States at the age of eighteen. She was an extremely poised and compliant woman—on the surface. However, her subservience was only a role that she played for others. Inwardly, she rebelled violently against everything that her family and her social background represented. This attitude was particularly evident when she was under the influence of alcohol. In fact, it was her inability to stop drinking that finally brought her to me. I might add here that Leila's physical and verbal assaultiveness (when she was inebriated) had led on two occasions to brief periods of confinement in the alcoholic ward of one of the city's hospitals.

In the beginning of my treatment of Leila, I attempted to aid her in uncovering some of the causes of her latent hostility and of her need to release pent-up feelings. She began to understand herself more clearly, and after a considerable period of time her over-all personality adjustment improved greatly. However, her addiction to alcohol remained the same. It was something that we were unable to change.

After quite a bit of thought, I finally decided upon a new therapeutic approach. I suggested that Leila do some volunteer hospital work assisting with patients in the same alcoholic ward to which she had been confined. I had two reasons for suggesting this. One was to confront her with the personality deterioration that is the consequence of continuous drinking. The other was to put Leila into a position that would make her feel important, needed, and looked up to by the other patients. I instructed her to play the role of the helping therapist with the other patients, though this was of course not her true title and function.

To my amazement and pleasant surprise, putting Leila into a role in which she was *helping others who suffered from the same problem that she had and who looked up to her* worked like magic, and enabled her finally to give up her own drinking. When last I heard, she had suffered no relapse.

The ease with which Leila was able to change made me very skeptical of the value of all *self-help* for those addicted to certain undesirable habits. Though Leila's case may of course not be typical, her cure seemed nevertheless to suggest to me a general principle that can perhaps be applied to other cases. Namely that not self-help but *"other-help"* is the way to break those inveterate habits of overindulgence that seem to be so difficult to shatter by oneself. Ultimately, I became convinced that the best (though perhaps not only) way to rid oneself of many harmful vices is not through an appeal to a mysterious will power, or through self-hypnosis, but by breaking the vicious cycle of individual habit formation *for, or* WITH, *some other person*. The principle of social facilitation and reinforcement, long recognized by psychologists in other areas of behavior, seemed to apply particularly to people who want to curb those desires and insatiable appetites that are to their own detriment. It is this principle that underlies the treatment procedure of *Alcoholics Anonymous*, and much of the success of that organization is probably due to the application of this method.

I tried to put into practice what I had learned theoretically, and it seemed to work. Instead of applying individual therapy, I organized patients who were addicted to certain undesirable habits into small groups and asked them to help others who were in the same or a similar predicament. In a sense it was like asking children to play the role of parents, or asking patients to become therapists for a while. Given this task and responsibility, most of the people I worked with were able to make at least a good start toward fighting their own difficulties.

It may interest you to know that I put Bert and Isabelle (the two patients mentioned previously) into the same therapeutic group. Bert's desire to help Isabelle and to set an example for her made him cut out the starches in his diet. By the same token, it was a challenge to Isabelle to try to "cure" Bert of his addiction by showing him how she herself could practice self-discipline and restraint in curbing her appetite. You might say, of course, that such treatment may only work for the duration of the therapy. However, what is so often most needed is to make a start in overcoming an addiction and then to go on from there toward further improvement.

I have given you the results of my own personal experience not in order to convince you of the value of group therapy or to bore you with the implications of a method, but to impress you with the importance of social motivation and incentive. If you want to smoke less, drink less, or eat less, though you may have neither the money nor the inclination for group therapy, you can practice its basic principles on your own. Help someone whose addiction is similar to yours to abstain, at the same time abstaining yourself. Conquer your vice together. Try doing volunteer or paid work with an organization that specializes in the prevention of or research in the addictions to which *you* are prone. Your private physician will be able to give you the names of such organizations. A call to the local chapter of the Red Cross, or to your local hospital could also be of help in this connection. The address of the central office of Alcoholics Anonymous in New York is 133 East 39th Street and the phone number is Oregon 9-3355.

As I have mentioned before, there is no perfect and quick cure, and I do not claim it. Your own experience in coming to terms with your problem, your physician's advice and treatment, your own willpower, and the fear of future complications that may arise from overindulgence, may be sufficient to help you overcome small or large addictions. However, if you have tried all these and the results have been of short duration or unfavorable, you may want to try some of the ideas which I have suggested in this chapter.

It has often been said that you must love someone else in order to receive love, that you must be interested in other people to be interesting. The idea that you must try to cure someone else to be cured yourself may apply with equal force. Try it and see how it works. Though it is not as simple as it may seem at first, it may be worth the effort.

CHAPTER 8

Fear of
Intellectual Inadequacy

Four main reasons why you *unnecessarily* feel stupid:

(1) *You lack formal education.* The number of people who believe themselves stupid or at least intellectually inferior because they are not academic degree holders comprises millions, I am sure. How wrong it is to assume that because you have not followed a prescribed course of academic studies, your powers to observe, to reason, and to learn are one iota less acute than those of people who have gone through the routine of an academic education. At the risk of repeating something that has been said many times, let me emphasize: college teaches a person how to use and broaden intelligence, *but it does not* create *more intelligence.* You leave the academic portals with the same intelligence rating that you had when you entered. The fact that you do not have a B.S. or a B.A. or have flunked out of school may be unfortunate, but you should not let this lower by one point your estimate of your own intelligence.

How can you establish your own intelligence? You do not always need a test, though such an examination can help to determine your I.Q. more precisely. Look back at the many situations in which you have been asked to learn new skills. The rate and accuracy with which you have been able to master them will give you an indication. Do you often see the essence of a story or current event more quickly than others? Do you catch on to a problem more readily than others? Are you curious about what makes things tick, the whys and hows? Has your practical judgment and foresight often been better or just as good as that of your fellow man? All these instances, and many other nonprofessional intellectual-ability tests that life administers to us without a fee, can be most important indicators of intellectual capability. They are often more revealing of intelligence than an academic degree, extensive formal education, or an I.Q. test.

(2) *You lack confidence because you are tongue-tied.* Quite a few individuals suffer inferiority feelings about their intelligence in social situations. Because they don't know the names of the latest best-sellers, because they are not glib talkers, or, in short, because they are not intellectual exhibitionists, they lack confidence in making use of their intellectual powers. If you don't have the confidence to talk and express yourself in company, your intelligence rating is lowered at least twenty-five points in the eyes of others. Eventually you come to believe that you yourself must be lacking somehow in gray matter because others always seem to have so much more to say.

This situation occurred in the case of an engineer who is one of the brightest men I know. Because he is the "strong, silent type" in company, he has the reputation of being unintelligent, and because of lack of recognition he has come to accept this verdict.

You should not let false modesty and underdeveloped social skills allow you to depress your intelligence in the eyes of others and ultimately in your own opinion. Do not be afraid to let others know how intelligent you are.

(3) *You look at the intelligence of others through a psychological magnifying glass.* The individual who is inferiority-ridden will view others as mental giants and look at himself as an intellectual dwarf. More than that, the psychological lens that throws his perception so much out of focus will make him think that others know more than he does, can reason out prob-

69

lems more effectively, and have all the answers at their finger tips. And once such an idea becomes lodged in one's unconscious mind, the distortion remains fixed. You can become firmly convinced that you are unintelligent because you overestimate the mental abilities of others.

Of course, just what "average" or "normal" intelligence is nobody knows for certain. Though it is rumored, as the result of extensive intelligence testing during World War I, that the mental ability of the average American is equivalent to that of a twelve-year-old child, this has been discredited by later psychological research. How you compare exactly with others in intelligence would be just as difficult to determine as counting the billions of nerve cells in your brain and comparing their number with those of every other person in the nation.

In view of the above, it is highly probable that you are not aware of how much you underestimate your own mental ability because to you the intelligence of others always seems so much better and more outstanding than yours.

(4) *You may not appreciate your unique brand of intelligence.* Just as there are different brands of soups and nuts, there are different kinds of intelligence. Though you may not possess the "standard" brand, your special variety of intelligence may be just as valuable.

Many of us associate intelligence exclusively with learnedness and professional status. Thus we often think that a doctor, teacher, or scholar *must* be intelligent. But we fail to recognize that the farmer who knows how to rotate a crop could be just as intelligent. In a similar vein, the housewife who has a knack for bringing the right people together at her dinner table exhibits a kind of intelligence that could be comparable to that of the brainy lawyer who decides upon the quality of a jury.

It is not sufficiently realized that psychologists, too, accept the fact that there is social intelligence, abstract intelligence, mechanical intelligence, verbal intelligence, arithmetical or mathematical intelligence, and quite a few others kinds of mental ability. Some individuals, of course, are smart in practically everything they do. However, most of us possess the kind of intelligence that is specialized to some extent. It is important, therefore, for you to recognize the area in which your intellect functions best. And don't underrate yourself if you find that you have the kind of mental ability which is special and may not be identical with what commonly goes under the stereotyped label of intelligence. You may have failed all of your mathematics tests, and yet put to shame the world's top mathematicians with the keen intellectual power that you apply in selecting horses for races or in arranging flowers in a vase.

However, I don't mean to imply that it is impossible for you to sharpen your mental abilities. In fact, your very doubts of intellectual ability could *serve as a special incentive to improve it.* The notion that a person's intelligence rating is fixed or must remain constant throughout life like some kind of birthmark has been abandoned by most psychologists (though this does not mean you can make a silk purse out of a sow's ear). It does signify, however, that most of us could learn how to enhance our intellectual powers. Some suggestions as to how to go about this follow.

Seek the company of bright people whenever possible. This does not mean that everybody who is going to be your friend from now on has to be a genius or that you will only associate with holders of the Phi Beta Kappa key. However, it does mean taking every opportunity to seek and enjoy the company of mentally alert, perceptive, and intellectually stimulating people. That some of their mental alertness is eventually bound to rub off on you stands to reason. It is interesting to observe in this connection that intelligent parents often have equally bright children, and most psychologists would attribute this to the influence of association and imitation and only to a minor degree of hereditary factors.

If you search among your acquaintances for people who have a variety of cultural and educational interests and are highly alert to what goes on in the world today, you will find more than you had first expected. Of course, I do not want to convey the impression that other qualities of personality are not of equal importance.

Observe more keenly. Ask more questions. Parents who are concerned with the improvement of their children's intellectual abilities usually tell them, "You must read more books and build up your vocabulary." However, such parents overlook that another and often better way of strengthening intellectual powers is by *keenly observing and questioning everything in one's immediate environment.* Such an attitude is characteristic of the very intelligent child who wants to know what makes the stars disappear in the daytime, what happens to flowers when they die, why shoes are made out of leather, why adults don't cry as often as children, and the answers to hundreds of other questions and problems. It is this continuous alertness of observation and curiosity in the child which lays the foundation for later wisdom, intelligence, and knowledge in the adult.

There is no reason why this searching, observing, and questioning attitude has to gradually die as we grow older. Therefore, if you feel that you want to enhance your intellect, wake up your perhaps dormant or grossly weakened perceptive capacities.

I once had the opportunity to meet with one of the world's leading scientists, considered a brain by everybody he came in contact with. As it happened, I was to welcome him at a railroad station. Since I was delayed, my friend had to wait at the station. When I finally arrived and offered my apologies to him, I was astonished and deeply impressed with how effectively he had used the time. Not only had he observed and analyzed some of the commuters and made guesses about their personalities, he could also give me a description of the architectural features of the place and, from conversation with one of the track hands, he already learned some of the characteristics of the town he was about to visit. In fact, he seemed to know more about it than I, who had been living there for quite some time! My contention is that this man may have been born with a highly developed intellectual potential but that its superior quality was constantly reinforced by his practiced powers of observation.

Is there any reason why *you* can not do the same with your intellectual capacity?

Establish new feelings of mental competence to replace habits of intellectual inadequacy. Most inferiority complexes are based on emotional experiences that have been burned into you painfully, like tattoo marks. The girl who has been made to feel ugly repeatedly during her childhood years finds it hard to believe that she is beautiful as an adult woman. Similarly, young people who have come to conceive of themselves as stupid will continue to carry this image of themselves, like an ineradicable mark, even if they earn applause and recognition for their intellectual achievements.

If you suffer from such a complex, you can only outgrow it through creating new and more positive *emotional* experiences which will gradually change your concept of your intellectual ability. Therefore learn to take full credit and bask in a victorious, pleasant feeling whether you have installed a new filing system in the office, designed a new dress, or shown ability in some area of your activities. Don't minimize your achievements in a neurotic way by saying: "*Anybody* could have done as well," or "I should have done it even *more* perfectly." The feeling of confidence and pride in your intellectual achievement, not of defeat and belittlement, must be built up systematically in you if you want to overcome an inferiority complex about your intelligence. In the same manner, try to win a discussion instead of conceding all of your opponent's points meekly and blaming it all on the shortcomings of your own arguments. Have the courage to risk failure in tackling difficult problems. Enter the arena of intellectual challenge like a bullfighter who knows the chance of defeat looms large but is willing to risk it. Perhaps this example is exaggerated, but only a radical departure from your previous emotional attitudes and approaches toward your own intellectual abilities will be able to lift the burden of inferiority which weighs down your efforts.

Realize that wisdom and creativity count as much as intelligence. In our achievement- and success-oriented society, the presence of intelligence—conceived of altogether too often as a tool for making more money and gathering more social prestige —is, in my opinion, widely overvalued. Our culture is too inclined to applaud and admire the bright man and woman and to fail to appreciate fully the wise and creative individual unless he or she makes the headlines.

As important as intelligence is *wisdom* (the ability to learn from emotional experience and to apply it to living), and *creativity* (the capacity to see life in a new and original manner and to communicate this to others). Sometimes these are combined with general intelligence. Psychological studies, however, have shown that this is not always the case, and many creative or wise people do not possess an excess amount of intelligence as we usually define it.

If you possess, at least to some degree, wisdom and creativity, many individuals with superior I.Q.'s may envy you for what you have, as you may envy them for the superiority of their intellectual capabilities.

Wisdom may be expressed by the way in which you live, by the kind of counsel and advice that you give to others, and by the goals that you establish for your future. You don't have to be a professional philosopher to be called "wise" or to live in a wise way.

Creativity may be expressed not only by painting pictures or writing books, but also by the originality that you apply to the daily tasks and relationships with which you are confronted.

CHAPTER **9** / Inability to
Make Decisions

Why is decision-making such an arduous task for some people? These individuals are thrown into a state of panic each time they have to choose between two or several alternatives. Here follow some examples of what happens to such "souls" who, as Dante recognized several hundred years ago "live without disgrace but also without praise and therefore are doomed to eternal suffering."

Mr. H., a business executive who thought he had "arrived" in the business world, encountered the following problem: Whenever he was called upon to make a crucial company decision, he was subject to a complete mental paralysis. He spent long hours in isolation, unable to make up his mind. He placed long-distance calls to get expert advice, and then cancelled them. He would pace up and down the floor, continually setting decision deadlines for himself which he could not meet; and finally he would retreat again into solitary meditation. When Mr. H. consulted me, he wanted me to make a man of decision out of him. In fact, his career was at stake unless he could overcome his indecisiveness.

❖   ❖   ❖

Margaret D. was advised by her physician to find a psychotherapist. Although she was given several referrals, she was unable to decide whom to choose. One doctor seemed too senile to her, another too infantile. A third impressed her as needing treatment himself. Everybody seemed to be lacking something. A whole year passed and she was still unable to make a choice. As the result of her chronic indecision she never received the help which she herself felt she needed desperately.

Though all of us sometimes vacillate when the time comes to choose or commit ourselves to some action, to many people indecisiveness is a pervasive and severely disabling pattern. If you detect a tendency toward indecision in yourself, what can you do to understand, recognize, and fight it?

Learn to face future consequences of negative decisions. Many individuals postpone making decisions because they are afraid of the consequences of a negative decision. The compulsive need of such people to be liked and loved by *everybody* is so strong that the anticipation of earning even the slightest disapproval robs them of the strength to act and to decide. Basically they are not really afraid to decide, but they fear a rejection as the result of their decisions. They must avoid rejection at any cost in order to maintain a self-image of importance.

Mr. J. consulted me because he could not decide whether or not he should let his teenage daughter go to Europe. Since he was overly attached to the young girl, refusing her wish meant to him that he was a "bad" father. He feared he might lose her love and affection and he was afraid to put his paternal foot down and say no. Rather than face such a horrible blow to his ego, he chose not to decide at all. He had had the same problem on his job where he always managed to get "sick" when it was necessary to discharge one of his subordinates or to voice some unfavorable criticism. Once he learned that saying no was not a crime and that even an unfavorable decision is, at times, welcomed by others, he found it much easier to act and to meet a crisis in a positive manner.

❉   ❉   ❉

Betty R. was a young woman who sought counseling because she could not decide whether to marry Tom, her fiancé. She had been engaged to him for three years. But as they got to know each other better, she began to realize that Tom was less mature than she had thought originally. When she found out that Tom had been unfaithful to her, she felt certain that they were not meant for each other. She even made a long list of Tom's assets and liabilities but could never balance them. Deep down in her heart she knew that she did not want to marry Tom, and she realized that she no longer loved him. However, there was something that kept her from facing the consequences of her feelings.

It was no coincidence that Betty had been brought up rather strictly by parents who taught her at an early age that a child should follow the principle of blind obediance in order to be loved and appreciated—and it was a lesson that she could never forget. In her relationship with Tom she could not definitely decide against marriage because she lacked courage and confidence in her own convictions.

What can you do if you are confronted with a similar dilemma and can't bear to face the consequences of a negative decision?

Recognize that others may not always be as sensitive to rejection and disapproval as you are. They may be able to face a negative decision with less pain and aggravation than you can.

Realize that we cannot help hurting the feelings of others at times, and we should not always blame ourselves for it. We can only try not to hurt others unnecessarily—or intentionally.

Keep in mind that the particular manner *in which you communicate a negative decision to others can greatly help to soften the blow that you strike.* You can say no in a firm yet friendly inoffensive manner.

Don't forget that as long as people basically *like and appreciate you, they won't mind an occasional refusal or rebuttal from you.* In fact, they may like you better for it, because they will think of you as being more honest and as possessing a "self" to respect. Thus, the child who loves his parents does not hate them when they disapprove, at times, of his actions. The person who says yes to *everything* is not truly liked.

If you are afraid to make negative decisions in important situations, gain the courage to make such decisions by "practicing" when the outcome of your decisions is not too crucial. Build up your ego by resisting the salesman who is trying to promote a product you don't really like. Learn to say no to the doorman who wants to get you a taxicab, if you really don't want him to. Once you have learned to make negative decisions in small things, you will find it easier to make up your mind when the issues involved are more important.

Every decision means giving up something. At the psychological root of our indecisiveness is the pleasure principle, which makes us wish for decisions that have *no disadvantages* at all. Unconsciously, we always want to have our cake and eat it too. We want to be rich without having to work for it, we want the emotional security of marriage without its responsibilities, or we desire luck and good fortune without previous risk. We are told that we have to work for what we get, but in reality we accept this unpleasant truth rather reluctantly. The part of us that has remained childish keeps on hoping that we can obtain *everything* without having to give anything.

| Let me tell you about Harold, a patient of mine who

was chronically indecisive. The source of his trouble was that he could not deny himself anything that was offered to him. As a popular and charming bachelor, he was never at a loss for invitations to parties and dinners. However, when they happened to fall at the same time, he was unable to decide which invitation to choose and which to reject. He dealt with this problem in a manner that was characteristic of his whole personality. He was compelled to accept *all* invitations. Thus, he would rush frantically from one party or dinner to the other, always offending his hosts by either leaving too early or arriving too late.

Once he received two invitations to spend the same weekend out of town. Undecided until the last minute as to which invitation to accept, he rushed to the railroad terminal, planning to take the first train that would take him to either one of his destinations. He thus avoided making a choice. When he arrived at the terminal, both trains had left and there were no others leaving the same day. His state of indecision resulted in a lonely weekend, as well as the hurt and anger of both his hosts.

Harold's problem was that he could not refuse appealing offers. This was not only reflected in his actions but was also manifest in his relationships with others. He had an address book that was filled to the brim with the telephone numbers of eligible young ladies, and he tried to accommodate all of them. However, though Harold never missed out on an opportunity for fun, he felt empty and unhappy most of the time.

If you are another Harold or find some of his traits in yourself, here are some helpful suggestions and thoughts on your problem. In making any choice, *the alternative that you have renounced will always appear more desirable to you.* The job that you did not choose will appear better than the one which

79

you decided to take. The invitation which you decided to accept will seem so much more dull and uninteresting than the party which you have chosen to forgo. The house that you bought will not be as good as the one which you decided against. However, you are operating under an illusion. Whatever we don't have, or don't choose, takes on a magic glow of unreality because fantasy tends to so glamorize the unknown that we forget to appreciate what we do have.

Though it is painful to give up something in a matter of choice, *it is often more aggravating to tolerate the anxiety of indecision.* Do you remember the last time you made up your mind definitely? Even though you may not have been entirely certain whether you acted wisely, didn't you feel gratified *after* you had made up your mind? Try to recapture this sense of intense satisfaction at having settled things once and for all, and you may not find it quite as difficult now to make decisions.

Try to get at the unconscious sources of your indecisiveness. If you have to make up your mind about something, you may think that you are fully conscious of the choices that are open to you. But you may be unable to reach a decision because the source of your conflict *is in your unconscious rather than in your conscious mind.*

As a woman you may find it difficult to choose between the purchase of two dresses. You may think that this is so because your taste is highly individual, or because you are very particular about clothes. Actually, your difficulty in deciding between the two dresses may be due to a variety of unconscious motives: the need to be conspicuous and the desire to conceal; the wish to spend recklessly and the need to save or conserve; the need to comply and appease (the sales person in this instance) and the wish to assert your own individuality. Of course, you do not always have to be completely aware of all these emotions. However, a knowledge of them is essential whenever you have to decide on vital issues.

Many of the unconscious reasons which block your capacity for making choices and decisions are unique and derive from your past personal experience. But there are two powerful unconscious determinants that operate in the decision-making process which are almost universal. One is the presence of a *too harsh and forbidding conscience*. The unconscious policeman in you can slap you down ruthlessly each time a decision comes up and you want to follow your intuition and natural impulses but can't. A little voice in you (perhaps reminiscent of that of your parents) says, "No, I forbid you to do it." The other unconscious reason for indecision is *overdependence upon the opinions of others*. If this is one of the causes for your anxiety, you will waver back and forth continually. Whatever decision you want to make will depend upon with whom you have been talking. You may rationalize this dependence by saying to yourself that you must get expert advice, you must consult others, you must gather every bit of evidence that is available before you are ready to decide. This, if applied within limits, is a good procedure for reaching a decision. However, many times it is merely a defense mechanism which you use to *avoid* or to *delay* the necessity for making a choice.

It seems that the best choices and decisions are those which we have made on the basis of our own *judgment and intuition*. Realize that *you* will have to live with the decisions that you make; the people who try to help you decide won't.

Though others may be superior to you in judgment, experience, and knowledge, there are certain significant feelings and attitudes which not even the closest relative, the best friend, or the most expert adviser can fully understand. The counsel of others when used as additional and valuable information may throw a new perspective on the decisions which you are about to make—but beyond this, *depend upon yourself*.

It is, of course, true that your intuition and judgment could turn out to be wrong, but even in such a case, you may need the *experience* of being wrong in order to learn how to make better and more appropriate choices in the future.

Many times you may merely *think* you are making your own decisions when they are actually someone else's. I have known patients who chose marital partners to please their parents, who entered occupational fields to satisfy a parental ambition, and who decided to "start a family" only to please a husband or wife. I was always amazed at how unaware these individuals were of the fact that such decisions were not their own, but were often the result of outside pressure from others.

Closely allied to an over dependence upon the opinions of others is the tendency to reach decisions on *the basis of values which are not your own*. You may, for instance, be advised by others to accept a certain job mainly because it carries much prestige. But you feel that prestige is not as important as the money involved, or vice versa. You may think that it is not wrong to marry outside of your religious faith, but your family and some of your friends may advise you strongly against it.

In these and other instances it seems important to realize that it would be better to base decisions on *your own individual values* instead of trying to depend upon those of others.

PART TWO

Sudden

Stresses

in Your Life

CHAPTER **10** / Job Loss

When you lose an important job suddenly or realize that you are on the brink of failing at work, an emergency exists. Why? Because a psychological source of activity, security, or challenge has been suddenly pulled right out from under you. This is an experience that is bound to produce some anxiety about your competence, your capabilities, and your future capacity to succeed.

Very often you are not told the *real* reasons why you are fired. "Reorganization," "change in methods and procedures," and "reduction in employment" can often be empty phrases and catchwords designed to cover up or to sugar-coat why it is *you* who must quit. You must not be deceived by phrases of this kind, but must try to find the deeper and more subtle causes for your discharge from work.

If, when you are fired, you are young and inexperienced in your occupation, you may feel particularly threatened because you lack the sense of reassurance that is derived from a past record of job success and achievement. If you are an older person, you may wonder whether you still possess the strength and flexibility to adjust to new employment, or whether you can find work in a labor market that is partial to younger employees. Regardless of age, being thrown out of work is comparable to being suddenly tossed into the ocean from a safe steamer. However, you must not lose your sense of direction or permit yourself to become confused.

In your present crisis, as in other emergencies, you can use positive and constructive or negative and destructive attempts to cope with the situation. Let me first point out to you some of the negative and destructive reaction patterns so you will be sure to recognize them in yourself and be able to avoid them whenever possible.

ESCAPE (RUNNING AWAY FROM IT ALL)

An escape may take the form of too long a vacation, of spending all your savings, or of overindulging yourself in various ways.

Such a runaway approach was used by a patient of mine who had lost a good job after twenty years of employment. Not feeling the pinch of dwindling financial resources because his wife earned a salary, he quickly succumbed to the life of a gentleman of leisure. It wasn't long before he formed habits such as getting up late, enjoying leisurely and expensive luncheons with other unemployed friends, and falling prey to excessive TV watching. Slowly, but persistently, he slipped into the role of the male "housewife," and came to look upon his wife as the bread-winner and provider for the family. Mild feelings of guilt about his unemployed status were taken care of by occasionally reading the want-ads (without following them up) and by griping about the poor conditions of the economy and blaming it for his unemployment. Finally, when he was called back to his former job, he amazed everyone by refusing it. Having had a taste of a life without responsibility, he was now unwilling and unable to give it up.

If you are a pleasure-seeking and self-indulgent person, you may be particularly prone to respond to unemployment as my patient did. However, don't misunderstand: You do need *some* fun and relaxation after the trauma of your job loss. But I would suggest that you put a definite time limit on your period of recuperation. Just as prolonged stays in rest camps proved to have ill effects on shell-shocked soldiers, removing yourself too long from *your* field of action (the labor market) could have disastrous consequences.

DISTORTION OF REALITY (FALSELY GLAMORIZING YOUR PAST JOB)

If your habitual reaction to stress and emergency is to regress, you may endow your previous job with advantages and satisfactions that are grossly distorted. You may indulge in reminiscences about the nice qualities of your boss and co-workers and berate yourself for not having appreciated them more, or think back to the reassurance of a regular paycheck. What you are apt to forget, on the other hand, are the many times when your conscientious efforts were ignored, or when you were reprimanded for mistakes that were really someone else's fault.

Looking at your past job through rose-colored glasses could be a dangerous tendency. It may have been a good job in many ways, but it was probably not as wonderful as it now appears to you in retrospective distortion.

PROJECTION (BLAMING YOUR PAST JOB EXCESSIVELY)

We all like to find a target that we can shoot at when we have been frustrated. Thus, sometimes people who have been fired wish in their fantasy to kill or injure the person who is responsible for the loss of a job. Perhaps your feelings may take the form of wishing to disgrace your former boss in public, or hoping he suffers a stroke, or wanting to see *him* fired from *his* job. As long as such wishes for revenge are confined to the realm of fantasy, they serve as a good outlet for pent-up resentment and hostility. Writing an angry and theatening letter to your boss may really help you to give vent to your feelings *provided that you never mail the letter!* Another way to release quite a bit of your hostility would be to verbalize your anger to close friends and relatives. However, try to restrain yourself from taking any *action that you may regret later.*

A case in point is that of a patient of mine who had lost a job with an insurance company which was known to have engaged in various unethical practices. Driven by intense anger about the injustice that he thought had been done to him, my patient needed a release for the discharge of his fury. The perfect opportunity for this lay in exposing the alleged unethical practices of his former company. In a frantic desire to get even with his former superiors, he initiated a lawsuit against them and hired a public relations man to expose the malpractices of the company. However, he underestimated the influential connections of his ex-employer and lost the suit. Later he came to regret the loss of time and money that could have been used more constructively in finding a new job for himself. What he had done helped to release anger temporarily, but it worked to his disadvantage in the long run.

It is obvious that all such reaction patterns are desperate attempts to place the blame for your job loss somewhere other than on yourself, as it is often more comforting to blame external circumstances. However, when we do this we always distort reality, often making futile and harmful attempts to correct past wrongs.

INTROJECTION (BLAMING YOURSELF TOO MUCH)

Just as feelings of anger and frustration can lead to undue

projection on the external environment, such feelings can also be excessively introjected, and thus result in a distortion of your own self-image. You will be particularly prone to introject your frustrations if you are the guilt-ridden, anxious kind of individual who has been subject to marked feelings of inadequacy and inferiority in the past. The loss of a job will then be the perfect cue for reviving old inferiority complexes which are now reinforced by your present experiences. Whatever competence and success you have attributed to yourself in the past will be blown to pieces at once by the impact of this new experience of rejection. Out of your past, the memories of failure and defeat will arise like ghosts and haunt you: the examinations that you failed in school; the times when you lost out in games and competition; the promotions which failed to materialize. Past success and positive achievement will shrink to nothing. You may not stop at this point. Your unconscious need for self-punishment may take the form of depriving yourself of every pleasure that comes up.

James H. lost his job. He immediately gave up all his social activities, cut out all his hobbies, and became quite miserly. Previously a generous and giving kind of person, he now put himself and his family on a tight budget and followed a rigid path of self-denial. At home he walked around in old clothes, ceased shaving, and spent long hours by himself brooding about his future. His unconscious need to punish himself and to relieve his feelings of guilt about having failed on the job became so intense that he soon lapsed into a deep depression which was further aggravated by his complete neglect of his outward appearance. When he finally forced himself to go to interviews with prospective employers, he made such a dismal and unfavorable impression that despite excellent qualifications no one wanted to hire him. Beyond that, his irritability and his unreasonably high demands made him so disliked by the employment agents that they soon refused to handle his case. Helpful suggestions from friends and acquaintances for finding employment were either rejected completely or met with angry counterarguments.

After you have gained some insight into these basically destructive and negative reaction patterns to a job crisis, you are in a better position to take a new and constructive approach to your own situation. This involves (1) a candid and critical analysis of the psychological reasons that may have motivated your dismissal (knowing why and where you failed may help you in your future career), (2) a constructive plan for future action which would lead to new and more successful employment experience.

PSYCHOLOGICAL CONSIDERATIONS WHY YOU FAILED ON YOUR JOB

The statistics of employment and personnel agencies indicate that the vast majority of job failures and dismissals are caused by personality factors rather than by a lack of knowledge or ability to perform the job. This is perfectly understandable if we realize that almost any work involves exposure to a certain amount of pressure, to criticism of some kind or other, and to varying degrees of competition. All these can be potential personality threats, often of the most subtle and yet devastating kind, for employment conditions that are characterized by perfect security, continuous appreciation of efforts, and complete fairness are hard to find anywhere. Since personality factors play such a large role in job failure, they will be discussed in greater detail below. Take a good look at some of the personality attitudes and see how much they may have characterized your own job behavior in the past.

You stress being "yourself" too much. The authors of many psychology books preach continually: "Be yourself! Be genuine. Try to express your *real* feelings and emotions. Only by being yourself can you succeed."

This is good advice as far as experience in your private life, your loves, and your friendships are concerned. However, on a job you cannot unconditionally follow the principle of "self-realization" without running into difficulty. Thus, as a working individual, it is often necessary to assume a role which is not necessarily identical with the one that you demonstrate at home, on vacations, or at a private party. This, of course, does not mean that you should be false or pretentious, but it signifies that on a job you cannot always give full and complete vent to your genuine feelings, desires and opinions as you would in your private life. The following examples may serve to illustrate this.

Jane's "private personality" may be described as that of an easygoing, blunt and carefree individual. The qualities which her friends admired in her were her complete frankness, her sense of humor (which she expressed in slightly risque stories), and her basic informality, reflected in her casual manner of dress, and indifference to the opinion of others. These were traits that she transferred unwittingly to her job. She worked in a rather large insurance company as assistant to the personnel manager, an older, conservative, unmarried woman who belonged to several highly respected clubs in town. Jane had always been an efficient worker and her superior intelligence, coupled with her speedy, efficient manner, made her highly respected by her co-workers. Jane thought, too, that her relationship with her supervisor was basically a good one, and she told this woman all about her dates, her successes at parties, and her weekend escapades. Jane knew what kind of clothes were most becoming to her and the tight sweaters or smartly cut sport shirts that she wore in the office earned her many admiring glances from the office clerks and the clients whom she interviewed.

At the company office party she danced with practically everyone, from the vice president to the truck drivers, and was delighted when the company's janitor, an older married man, escorted her home in a taxicab. To her great surprise, Jane was fired after only several months of employment. Flabbergasted by the suddenness of her dismissal from work (allegedly because of occasional lateness for work), she learned later that her success with men and what was referred to as her "general lack of dignity" had aroused the intense contempt and perhaps envy of her supervisor. This was the real reason she was fired.

*　　*　　*

Sid held a job as a clerk in an advertising agency and he was tremendously popular. There were two reasons for this. First, his repertoire of funny stories and jokes delivered during lunch hour held everyone spellbound. Second, when it came to clowning and performing, Sid was often compared to some of the top comedians by his co-workers. He earned the same kind of reputation at work that he had at home where his jokes and his comical performances made him the center of attraction. Although Sid impressed people as a "clown," he was at the same time a serious and ambitious person. However, he usually repressed this aspect of his personality at work. He continued to play the part of the cute little boy, a role that had been encouraged by his family who hated to see him grow up to adult status and responsibility. Although Sid's gay and carefree manner earned him the attention he had always craved, most of his co-workers and supervisors actually had little respect for him. He did not give them the opportunity to observe that he *could* be mature and responsible.

Sid became almost tragically aware of this when a reorganization of the company presented an opportunity for advancement. The promotion to administrative assistant which Sid had been eager to get was refused him, because management felt that his office personality was too immature to place him in a position of enhanced responsibility. With a sudden flash of insight it then became clear to Sid that he had overplayed the role of the clown, and though his family loved him for his boyish charm and exuberance, this side of his personality was not the one to be stressed at work. Unfortunately this insight came too late, and the impression that he made at work had become so fixed in the eyes of his supervisors that they failed to realize he had potentials which could have qualified him for more responsible work.

You are too compliant. In many situations compliance is a virtue; in fact, we often like compliant people because they don't threaten us and they somehow strengthen our own sense of power and superiority. Furthermore, compliance is a trait that has been drilled into us as children by our parents, and therefore is often hard to shake off as adults.

However, *excessive* compliance at work, particularly when it becomes a rigid and pervasive reaction pattern in job relationships, may lead to contempt and exploitation.

In a society that puts a strong emphasis on the self-made and "go-getter" sort of individual, the overly agreeable and compliant person is often looked down on as weak, unoriginal, and inferior. Though the work of quiet, inconspicuously efficient, and subordinate individuals is the backbone of many business organizations, such people are often ignored when it comes to salary raises and promotions. This is so because the employee who is always willing to comply with the demands of his superiors may unwittingly lower the value and price of his own services. His good-natured compliance can easily be mistaken for stupidity or lack of judgment; while the worker who voices opposition occasionally and is more aggressive may be resented temporarily, but is often more appreciated in the long run, for he creates the image of the future executive.

The deeper psychological causes of an attitude of over-compliance are (1) overly strict parents, (2) unpleasantness and reversals in childhood when self-assertion was shown, (3) defensive needs to please in order to gain safety and approval. As a result of these causes, a compliant child often grows into a compliant adult and attitudes previously displayed toward family members are now transferred toward the parent substitutes —in this case, superiors or authority figures in the world of work. Once you recognize your superiors at work are not replicas of your father or mother, and that you don't have to hang on to their approval the way a child clings to a parent, you will have taken an important step toward overcoming your overcompliance at work.

You tend to be too critical. Just as an overdose of compliance can ruin you at work, overdoing the role of the critic and judge on a job can lead to disaster, and in the more serious instances, to dismissal. The following job situation, brought to my attention by one of my patients, seems to be a perfect example of this.

> Arlene F. worked as an executive secretary in a large advertising agency. Mr. Mark, her boss, was a very intelligent and resourceful but also a very forgetful and high-strung man, who hated to be bothered with office details. Arlene was his "walking conscience." Whenever Mr. Mark failed to sign letters, forgot to return business calls, or showed up too late for appointments, Arlene was there to remind him of his shortcomings. The young woman was efficiency personified and thought that her orderliness and keen sense of responsibility made her extremely valuable to her boss. She justified her actions by assuming that they were in the best interest of her company, even though her

frequent criticism and the manner in which she expressed it were often a source of irritation to Mr. Mark.

All was well, however, till Arlene left for her well-deserved vacation and another secretary was hired as her temporary replacement. Arlene's substitute, Susan S., was a warm, friendly girl with a special flair for saying just the right thing at the right time. Though she realized Mr. Mark's shortcomings, she rarely pointed them out to him directly. Soon she had gained her superior's confidence because she was willing to listen attentively to some of the home problems that kept Mr. Mark from giving his full attention to his work. Susan was not as efficient as Arlene in some respects, but her role as a confessor made Mr. Mark more relaxed and thus indirectly she helped him to keep his mind on his work. She learned to correct some of the errors that occurred on the job almost without his being aware of it. The unfortunate outcome of this situation was that when Arlene returned from her vacation, it was Susan who was kept on the job. Arlene, though she was the more efficient secretary, was gradually eased out of the job.

Arlene's mistake, being overcritical at the wrong time, is repeated many times in the business world. Though a critical attitude is often desirable, it must be used with the utmost tact and discretion in an employment situation.

Most business organizations claim that they want employees who are not automatons, but have minds of their own and can come up with criticism and new ideas. But when an employee gives vent to his critical impulses, he may find himself more ostracized and rebuffed than appreciated. Since too much criticism on the job can easily earn you the reputation of being a chronic griper and complainer, I would suggest application of the following rules if you *must* criticize: (1) Express your criticism only to the individual who might be able to correct an existing fault, not to others who will merely pass it on in a distorted form. (2) Avoid *personal* criticism whenever you can, although it may be intended to help and you think it is constructive. Most people cannot bear to have others point out their personal shortcomings. (3) Resist the urge to criticize *immediately* and save your comments for the right time and the right moments. The person whom you approach may not listen to you when he is busy or under duress, but he may lend an ear to your observations or complaints when he is not busy and others are not around to witness and perhaps agree with what you have to say.

You tend to be too detached emotionally. Undoubtedly you have met detached people. Such individuals are almost always friendly and courteous, but their distant and reserved attitude makes it hard to tell what they really think and feel. The deeper and often unconscious philosophy of a detached person is: "If I withdraw emotionally into a shell of isolation I cannot get hurt or misunderstood. Therefore it is always, and under all circumstances, wiser to keep my real feelings to myself."

Although, as was pointed out before, it is unwise to give unlimited vent to your feelings in a job environment, it is wrong, too, to adopt a completely detached attitude. You may earn a certain amount of respect this way, but you will never be really liked and appreciated if you keep ninety-nine per cent of your genuine feelings under lock and key. Thus, even an occasional and inappropriate temper outburst will be forgiven and understood, but an attitude of complete emotional detachment will only arouse suspicion in your co-workers, supervisors, and subordinates.

If detachment is one of your characteristic ways of dealing with people, it would be to your advantage to try to overcome this attitude at work. How?

Try to let people know that you, too, are subject to errors and faults. Admit on occasion that you have moods, shortcomings, and a desire to be liked and appreciated like everyone else. Learn to laugh and to applaud warmly at jokes. Attempt not to be bored or indifferent when others tell you their problems.

Don't close your eyes and ears to some of the subtle ways your colleagues use to establish a closer relationship. Recognize and acknowledge clearly and unmistakenly small favors and extra courtesies that are extended to you.

Even if you think that you are aware of the more personal feelings and needs of others at work, this awareness needs to be expressed verbally and communicated clearly.

Don't be too perfectionistic. If you are a perfectionist, your need to work at the maximum level of your efficiency can become so blind and obsessive that it could drive you to a nervous breakdown or a stomach ulcer.

Thus, the supervisor who is an unreasonable perfectionist will find cause for annoyance and anger wherever he looks. His blood pressure will go up if the receptionist comes in two minutes late. Throughout the day he will look for instant and perfect attention to his commands even if circumstances make this impossible. He will rewrite his own memos one hundred times because they don't express *exactly* what he wants them to say. Justifying his own perfectionism under the cloak of efficiency, he cannot see that a little less indefectibility could result in greater productivity, and in more job satisfaction on his part.

Just as the boss may expect too much perfection from his employees, they, in turn, may project their perfectionist needs by anticipating faultlessness from their superiors and hating them if their anticipations are not fulfilled. Thus, some may conceive of a leader of a business organization as strong as a good father, as insightful as a psychiatrist, and as composed and wise as a Buddhist priest.

If he deviates only one iota from this projected and highly idealized image, the perfectionist will resent him.

Learning how to overcome conscious and unconscious perfectionist tendencies is a difficult task. Perhaps a first step toward improvement is to recognize that the psychological roots of excess perfectionism are often manifestations of displaced hostility and resentment. In other words, continuous demands for perfection from others may be a disguised way of expressing hostility toward them. Perfectionism can also stem from an unreasonable fear of future failure that makes for dissatisfaction in *any* job. In either case, knowing and understanding some of the reasons for your excess need to be perfect should help you to control this trait, or at least to temper its intensity.

HOW TO FORGET THE BAD PAST AND PREPARE FOR A GOOD FUTURE

These, then, are some of the reasons that may have been responsible for your failure in previous employment. After you have thoroughly analyzed them and have learned from your past mistakes, all your efforts and thoughts should be bent toward the *future* and, more specifically, toward getting a new and more suitable job. Here are a few suggestions in regard to this problem.

In job hunting it is of utmost importance to know beforehand the kind of job that you want, and to realize what you are willing to accept or to reject in the way of employment. If you leave the choice of job to employer or employment agent, he is likely to resent the additional burden that, by being vague and indecisive, you place upon him.

If you are undecided whether you should stay with the kind of work you have been doing so far, seek professional assistance by taking tests in a vocational guidance agency, or by consulting a psychologist who specializes in occupational guidance. However, don't expect that the mere taking of aptitude tests will solve all your problems. What counts is the quality of the counseling connected with the testing, and your counselor's ingenuity in spotting your unique job problem. To do this he must be able to utilize the sum total of his professional and life experience. Unfortunately, there are many poor tests and not all counselors are good. The best way to find a good vocational counselor is to go to someone who has been personally recommended to you or, if this is impossible, to seek the services of a guidance agency that is connected with a reputable college or university. After you have decided to seek such help, prepare your interviews and counseling sessions by doing some thinking and exploring on your own *beforehand,* and you will get more out of them.

In order to locate a specific job, don't hesitate to make extensive use of personal contacts and connections. Before you resort to newspaper ads and employment agencies, compile an extensive list of friends and even casual acquaintances who may be of potential value in your job-hunting campaign. Bury false pride and realize that often they will feel superior if they can be of assistance to you. If they can't, they will tell you frankly, and not hold your effort against you. However, one word of caution: in your present job crisis try not to fall back on employment with a company that is owned or managed by members of your family. For it is only in rare instances and on a temporary basis that such an arrangement is satisfactory. Thus, although your father may have your interests at heart, his ideas for work and success may differ widely from yours. Similarly, your wife's or husband's family may love you dearly as a person, but working with them in a business may introduce problems and complications that could wreck your marital relationship.

When you are eventually called for an employment interview, size up the person who sees you as well as you are able and vary your approach in accordance with this impression. During your initial interview, your prospective employer may want you to do all the talking, or he may love to lecture to you himself. Be flexible and refrain from adopting extreme attitudes of overcompliance, overconfidence, false modesty, or overfamiliarity. Have the courage to be different than you expected to be during an interview, should the situation call for it.

If a job is offered to you and you have doubts whether to accept or reject it, weigh personality factors and initial impressions before you make a decision. If you already feel at this point that you would dislike most of the people with whom you would be working, and that there is something in the work atmosphere that repels you, no amount of job prestige or salary will ultimately compensate you for these negative feelings. Furthermore, don't take a job merely because *others (but not yourself)* think it is suitable for you or because it has an attractive title.

CHAPTER 11 / Death of a
Loved One

No matter how complicated a relationship, how heart-breaking a disappointment, how much physical or mental suffering life involves, there is a thread of hope for the sufferer, sometimes barely perceptible, but present nevertheless. And there are words of advice and consolation that, though they cannot cure, may yet act as a soothing sedative for him. However, when a person who has been close to us dies, "is pushed into eternal silence," as the poet Rilke says, it seems like an almost hopeless task to console the bereaved. The words which are said often ring stale and flat. I hope that, in spite of the shortcomings of language, some important thoughts, feelings, and ideas will find their way to you in this chapter. The following are a few suggestions that I would offer to you had you lost a close family member or friend through death and come to me for counsel and emotional support.

Try to give vent to your feelings instead of repressing them. This is essential. Though your first reaction may be one of numbness and shock that inhibits you, try to counteract your desire to restrain. Grief and sadness will only rise to the surface with greater pain if held back too long. Even some scientific evidence indicates that it is better to release your feelings than to repress them in situations of personal loss and bereavement.

An outstanding psychiatrist who has observed hundreds of

101

bereaved patients, discovered that those who held back their overt expressions of sorrow later developed more severe depressions and physical symptoms (such as stomach ulcers and cardiac neuroses) than those who released their emotions.

The outward expression of your grief may take many different forms; but regardless of how other people mourn, you must express your sorrow in the way that is most natural to you. But express it you must. Do not internalize your sorrow; do not hesitate to speak of it frequently to others. Although it may be difficult and painful to do so at first, it will eventually serve to alleviate your mourning.

Realize that depressions and loss of interest are to be expected but will pass in time. Your depression may take the form of an almost complete loss of interest in everything but the person who has passed away. You may want to do nothing but brood and be by yourself. Your depression could also manifest itself indirectly through an increased irritability and a seemingly hostile reaction toward your family and those who are trying to console you. Many trivial arguments often take place in families where a death has occurred. Be aware of the fact that such quibbling and fighting should not be taken too seriously because it merely represents another way of discharging tension and grief. There is no real animosity between you.

The feeling of gloom that you experience now is natural. It would be futile for anyone to try to talk you out of it. But what you *can* do under the present circumstances is to make every effort to *avoid situations that provoke or enhance depression.* Spending long evenings by yourself, listening to sad music, reminiscing over old pictures are examples of such situations.

Don't be surprised if for a while you are unable to concentrate on anything for any length of time. Your thoughts and feelings naturally drift back to the image of the deceased person.

The only way to cope with your present confusion is to

realize that it is *temporary*, though at present you cannot imagine that you will ever be free of grief.

Don't make important changes in your way of living till you feel ready for them. You may find it necessary to alter your present pattern of living. This is particularly true if the person who passed away was a family member upon whom you strongly depended. You may be faced with severe financial problems which force you to move from your present home and change your whole style of living. To make the right decisions will take time and careful thought. Whatever you do, try not to rush into anything prematurely under the pressure of the circumstances.

Friends and well-meaning acquaintances tend to make many suggestions to keep you occupied in order to help you over your crisis. In their desire to aid you, they want you to meet more and new people, and seek more diversion. They even force their own company upon you when you want to be alone. Of course you may, in your present crisis, need an outside push to get over your lethargy and despair. However, such a push, if acted on *while you are still very vulnerable* to feelings of depression, might only result in a relapse later on.

Be aware that relapses can occur after you begin to feel better. After a few weeks or months you may suddenly feel better and more optimistic about everything. In fact, you may almost think that the worst has passed and that you are over the hump. Others will compliment you about the change in your outlook and attitude. They themselves will be happier and relieved not having to worry about your state of mind. It seems almost as if you are finally ready to make a new start in life. Then suddenly something happens that upsets your emotional equilibrium. Any minor incident can cause this. It may be triggered by meeting someone who was a close friend of the person who died, or by the arrival of a letter addressed to the deceased individual as though he were still alive. When such incidents occur, the emotional wound you thought was beginning to heal breaks wide open again. All the progress you felt you had made toward recovery is wiped out in one stroke. You find yourself regressing completely to the hopeless state that you were in weeks or months ago.

Emotional relapses of this kind will occur again and again. You can only get over them by realizing that they will be less frequent and less painful in the future. You must not allow them to discourage you. Anticipate them and they will hurt less.

Don't give in to false feelings of guilt. In everyday life some feelings of guilt are normal, conscious, and correctable and can be traced back to definite actions. The individual who feels guilty suffers for some time but can be relieved from this suffering by recognizing its causes and trying to make up for his "sins."

However, the guilt feelings that arise in those who survive a loved one are more painful because there is no way to make up for past wrongdoing or insufficient kindness. Such individuals feel that they should have been *more* kind, *more* loving, *more* understanding, and *more* tolerant of the faults of the deceased person.

In every human relationship there is something that could have been done better, some unfulfilled potential. And it is this unrealized potential that makes us feel despondent. If the person whom we think we have failed is still alive, we can rush to the phone or write and say: "I was wrong, I've made a mistake. I did not know what I was doing. Please forgive me." In most instances it is possible to relieve our guilt this way. However, if feelings of remorse seize us when a person had died, the words that we want to say to ask forgiveness can never be heard.

A woman whose husband had died several months before consulted me because she had been suffering from a severely disabling depression and seemingly incurable insomnia. Her husband had died as the result of a heart

104

attack which had been predicted by his physician. The doctor had advised him to avoid emotionally trying situations. This, of course, was a prescription that was difficult to follow. It was particularly difficult for this man because he was highly excitable and very sensitive. One day he had a minor argument with his wife, and shortly after this he succumbed to a fatal heart attack. It is easy to see how the man's wife blamed herself for what had happened. Though any other upsetting or frustrating situation could have been the cause of his death, she took all the blame for it.

In treatment it became apparent that this woman harbored strong feelings of hostility toward her father and felt guilty because of them. Her father had died as the result of an accident for which my patient also held herself responsible. Later, the experience of her husband's death revived the previously repressed feelings of guilt about her father's death. It took her a long time to adjust intellectually to the source of her guilt, and even longer to accept it emotionally. However, once she did gain some insight into their causes, her symptoms of depression and insomnia began to subside.

This, of course, is an extreme case, and the sources of guilt toward people who have died are often less clear or obvious. Yet strong and often unwarranted feelings of guilt do play a large part in our reactions to people who have died. They are often the cause of depressions. It is as if the depressed person is denying himself pleasures and adopting a continuous state of gloom because he hopes to relieve his feelings of guilt this way.

If you are experiencing such feelings now, you may be *imagining* that you were not the kind of son, daughter, husband, wife, parent, or friend that you always wanted to be. All of us form idealized images of the roles that we should play in human

105

relationships, and there are moments when we come close to the fulfillment of these images. But at other times we fail miserably. Then we are like actors who have not responded to the right cues, or who under emotional pressure, merely repeat lines instead of expressing what is really felt and experienced.

If you have a good reason to suspect that you failed the person who died, guilt about this may be grossly distorted and exaggerated under the impact of death. It is very likely that you endow the individual who has passed away with a halo that is not real. The famous quotation: *"De mortuis nil nisi bonum,"* (of the dead, think only good), is a statement that has survived from the time of the ancient Romans. Such positive distortion can, however, enchance your feelings of guilt by magnifying the virtues of the deceased person as well as your own shortcomings.

Tell yourself that whatever hurt you have inflicted may *not* have gone as deep as you think. Your loved one also received your love and understanding, though it may never have been verbalized.

Realize that self-pity is not the solution. A certain amount of self-pity can help, but if you now make a fetish out of it and indulge in it excessively you may prolong your sorrow and unhappiness unnecessarily. Just as our pride is hurt when others pity us, when we pity ourselves it leaves a bad taste in our mouths, so to speak. When we ask for pity from others, we make emotional beggars of ourselves, and really indicate that we have given up hope for earning more rewarding love and admiration. In a similar way, when you settle for self-pity you are degrading and weakening your own self-image. Self-pity, too, is harmful because it can rob you of almost all your energy and paralyze your capacity for constructive thought.

A better and more satisfactory attitude than self-pity could be one of *nobility and strength* in coping with the inevitable. This, of course, does not mean that you should repress your bereavement and hide your grief under a mask of pretended de-

tachment and dignity. It does mean, however, that you want to
rise, not fall, with the tragic situation that has occurred.

Religion can aid you in gaining such a feeling of strength
and nobility. Or you may find it helpful to think of the example
of individuals who have, with strength and admirable courage,
gone through similar experiences. Close identification with them
will make you feel stronger yourself. For example, a patient of
mine whose husband died at about the time of the assassination
of President Kennedy was helped in bearing her own grief with
greater fortitude after she had watched the serene, courageous
manner in which the late President's wife conducted herself during the funeral.

Don't neglect the future meaning of your life. If your life
has been centered very closely around the person who passed
away, your future will seem to have lost its deeper meaning and
significance. Life is worthless unless there is some meaning, purpose, and goal to it. There are two considerations that may help
you to regain a sense of meaning in life. One of them is linked to
the past, the other to the future.

Though the person who has left your life is not with you
any more, your life could now become more meaningful if you
consider yourself a living representative of his goals and ideals.
Of course, you would not want to mold your own life entirely in
accordance with the past, but there are many large and small
ways in which you could continue to follow up and perhaps complete what the person who died had left undone.

The second way in which you could gradually rediscover
life's lost meaning is *by being wide open to new and different
patterns of experience.* Realize that every new life situation,
though it may be disadvantageous at first, also has certain advantages. Having lost one member of a family, for instance, may
bring you closer to someone whom you may have neglected before. Being forced to become independent after a period of
prolonged dependency upon someone else could uncover new

strength in your character that you never knew you had. History abounds with the examples of men and women who led satisfactory and productive lives even after they suffered the loss of the person to whom they were most close. Like yourself, at first they usually thought that they could not continue on their own, but they did and succeeded.

CHAPTER **12** / Divorce

IF YOU ARE A DIVORCÉE . . .

Accept your social self without status anxiety. Too many women feel socially self-conscious because they are divorced. They have the uncomfortable sense that people automatically label them "divorcée," and therefore have preconceived ideas concerning them. If this is your feeling too, try to realize that such prejudice on the part of others is most often a product of your own imagination. Although there are some people who are biased against divorce, if you act relaxed and natural when in company, the majority won't be judging you by your marital status. No matter what the circumstances of your divorce, being a divorcée is nothing to be ashamed of. Yours may even be a case meriting congratulations, for perhaps you displayed courage and maturity in breaking up a destructive relationship.

As a recent divorcée you may now find that you are perfect prey for sexual advances from your single (and sometimes married) male friends and acquaintances. Don't become too alarmed if this happens. If you are not interested, learn to refuse their advances gracefully and with a minimum of anger. Only a woman who feels grossly inadequate about herself as a person will be offended by a man's sexual advances, and fail to credit herself with other attractions besides sex appeal. Think twice before you cast aside a potential friend or date, and remember, too, that to a large extent *you* are the one who sets the pace and pattern of a future relationship with a man.

The kind of love life you want to lead will now depend largely upon your already established code of morals. Should your upbringing make it impossible for you to accept sexual relationships without marriage or the definite prospect of it, you should probably abstain, because the ensuing guilt feelings are likely to be too intense. On the other hand, if you can accept extramarital sex relationships without too much guilt, with discrimination, and with discretion, you should not worry about your reputation. Nevertheless, it would be wise to keep in mind that an affair may get you more deeply involved emotionally than you might wish to be under your present circumstances.

Take a job if you are not working already. Although your divorce may have undermined your sense of financial security, realize that nowadays marriage is not the only way in which a woman can provide a nest egg for her future. This is borne out by the fact that many women hold jobs which provide them not only with a present but also a future source of income. Regardless of economic necessity, however, most divorced women feel that engagement in some kind of work (going to school or taking a job) has helped them considerably in making the difficult transition from married to unmarried existence. You too may come to this conclusion. Perhaps you are worried that some of your educational and vocational skills may have become somewhat rusty. Well, they usually come back quickly if the motivation "to learn and to earn" is there. You need not go back to the job you may have held before "He" came along and tied the marital knot. New and different opportunities of employment for women may have arisen since the time when you received your last salary.

Give careful thought to any plans for moving back in with your family. Avoid such a step if you can. Going back home to the folks could be a strong temptation now, if you have little or no money, have never lived by yourself, or if that psychological umbilical cord has never really been cut. There are several problems inherent in this return-to-the-home-base arrangement. To begin with, your parents (despite their assurances to the contrary) may continue to look upon you as a child, instead of as an adult woman. Worse than that, in many instances *they will continue to treat you as a child,* ruling your life and expecting you to "do in Rome as the Romans do." Second, settling down now to the comforts and conveniences of your old family life may make you so fat and lazy that in time you lose almost all of the zest and energy it takes to build a new life of your own. Of course, living with your parents will give you comfort, care, and convenience, and could save you quite a bit of money. However, in exchange you may sacrifice two precious prerogatives: freedom and independence.

Don't run back to your husband at the slightest provocation. Perhaps you are still very much in love with your previous mate—in spite of the divorce. There may be moments when just hearing the voice of your *ex* over the phone could send you right back into his arms. Such moments, however, are dangerous in that they might lead you to premature reconciliation with him. Therefore, if the all-is-forgotten-and-forgiven impulse seizes you suddenly, counteract it with such thoughts as these: (1) Time and physical separation are not enough to wipe out basic personality differences. Certainly, returning to your husband now might be like a second honeymoon. But only for a while. It would probably not take too long for the old arguments and differences to be revived. (2) Promises made under pressure are often not kept. He may swear now that he will never touch another drop of alcohol, never look at another woman, never give in to his family, or stay out too late on weekends. But can you be certain that this sudden transformation of character will last? Only time can tell, and trusting his promises now may be disastrous.

If you have children in your custody, don't expect too much of them. Love them wisely, *not possessively.* This is not an

111

easy task for you, I know. You may wish to center all your life around them, or perhaps unconsciously use the "poor darlings" to make up for your previous disappointment or frustration in marriage. In an eagerness that may be partly triggered by feelings of guilt and partly determined by resentment of your former husband, you may try too hard to play the role of the missing father.

Have a life of your own. Don't live exclusively through your children, trying to make them achieve what was denied to you. If you make too many sacrifices for your children, you will also expect too much of them in return, and will only be disappointed if, when they mature, they do not give back to you in affection and achievement what you earlier invested in them emotionally. Remember, the more you fulfill your own needs, and the less frustrated you are as a woman and a person, the better it will be for your children in the long run.

Keep in mind that although it may be unfortunate for *any* child to have to grow up without the regular presence of a father, you should not try to replace him. Let your child find his or her own father-substitute. He may do this by forming a strong attachment or admiration for an uncle, a neighbor, a teacher, a grandfather, or any other fatherly figure. Although the physical presence of a father is, of course, most essential for the process of child development, his absence or only occasional presence in a family structure does not always need to spell disaster and misfortune.

The foregoing is certainly not an appeal to be self-indulgent and irresponsible toward your child. Caring for a child and watching his development can give your life meaning and purpose—now and in the future. It is important that you love your child in a wise and mature way, and that you try to recognize the mistakes that led to the breakup of your marriage and avoid their repetition.

Be careful how you discuss your divorce with your child or children. Just what and how much you say about the reasons for your divorce will be an important test of your emotional maturity and it will take much wisdom and restraint on your part to handle this situation in the right way. You especially want to avoid two errors: telling your child *too much* or *too little* about what has happened between you and your husband. If you err in the direction of telling him too much, perhaps suggesting that Daddy and you just *never* saw eye to eye, or that he had always been cruel and selfish, you may destroy your child's basic faith in the institution of marriage and distort his image of the male. You may, by telling your child too much, induce what psychologists call a childhood trauma. You are particularly prone to mistakes of this kind if you yourself feel very insecure about your child's love for you, and are therefore trying to draw him closer by negative distortion of the father image. If, on the other hand, you tell too little about the divorce, thinking that the child is too young or immature to understand, you may leave him exposed to his own doubts and confusion. He may then have to make his own evaluation of your marriage (which he *is* too young to do). It would be wrong, for example, to say "We are going to live without Daddy for a while because he has gone on a trip," and let it go at that. Besides, there is a good possibility that your child has noticed for a long time before the divorce that things weren't as they should be between you and your husband, though he may not have talked to you about it.

A guiding principle for such a situation may be to tell as much of the truth (without vituperation or belittlement of your husband) as you think your child can understand, depending upon his age and emotional maturity. Perhaps you should point out to him in this connection that just because your marriage did not work out does not mean that there is something wrong with *all* marriages. Also, tell him that just because you and his father are now divorced does not mean that Father will love and care less for him than he has in the past.

Be aware of the fact that your child's resentment of the divorce may be expressed indirectly. It could manifest itself by increased irritation and rebellion against you, particularly when you ask him to do things that he thinks his father should tell him to do. Or your child could project his disappointment at the dissolution of your marriage by loving you less *for a while* and becoming more resentful of you. Realize that such resentment is a natural expression of his conflicting emotions, and is usually temporary. If you refuse to become too seriously offended and try to give your child more, rather than less love, you will be building a happier future relationship between you.

Another problem that takes wise handling involves setting the balance between being a good mother and making up for the absence of a father's influence. Try not to go to an extreme in this respect by becoming overly tough or demanding, or applying methods of discipline that are alien to your own personality. If you suddenly shout (as perhaps your husband did) when you want Junior to go to bed, or want him to stop watching television, the raised pitch in your voice will not be enough to give you paternal authority. Your goals for the child may be the same as those of your former husband (provided they were sound), but you must find your own methods of applying them to your child.*

IF YOU ARE A DIVORCÉ . . .

How you adjust psychologically to your divorce will, of course, depend to a considerable extent upon individual circumstances. If your wife has deserted you or has fallen in love with someone else, you may be subject to severe doubts about yourself and about your masculinity. Try to remember that your view of the situation is distorted at this point (as in any crisis or emer-

---

*For further information on the handling of children in the divorce situation, read *Children of Divorce* by Louise J. Depsert, Doubleday & Company, Inc., 1963; *Stepchild in the Family* by Anne W. Simon, The Odyssey Press, 1964; *What to Tell Your Child* by Helen S. Arnstein and Alfred Buckmueller, Bobbs-Merrill, 1962.

gency). The appearance of your present inferiority complex could merely be a revival of long buried experiences, as when you feared the loss of your parents' love, or when you lost out in competition with a more successful brother or sister. Make sure, therefore, you do not *overreact* because of *past* situations.

With regard to the more immediate and concrete adjustment problems which confront the male divorcé, the following suggestions may be helpful:

When divorce meaningfully reduces your financial resources . . . . Paying your wife alimony can, of course, do away with a considerable portion of your paycheck. The financial adjustment to divorce may make it necessary to revise many of your daily habits and to lower your standard of living. It is most natural that you feel hurt and, more than that, disgusted when your paycheck (already reduced by tax deductions) is further substantially shrunk by your monthly alimony. To make matters worse, most of the time you have little or no jurisdiction over how the money that you send to your ex-wife is going to be used. However, aggravating yourself will only lead to *more* aggravation. Try to look at your financial situation this way: even if you did not have to pay alimony, not all of the money saved would be put to wise use. Another consideration: fulfilling your financial obligations to your ex-wife may help you to feel less guilty about the divorce.

In the beginning you can expect quite a bit of difficulty in making ends meet. However, gradually you will find that there is a good bit of honest wisdom in the cliché that "money isn't everything." If you go out socially, you may discover that spending less money on entertaining does not necessarily mean that you enjoy yourself less or receive less love and affection. Try viewing the need to budget and cut corners here and there as somewhat of a challenge to your financial ingenuity and organizing ability. And, last but not least, there is always the hope that your divorced wife may remarry and relieve the drain on your wallet.

Pick up your life where you left it before you were married. Make a fresh start! Your years of married life may have gotten you so accustomed to a home routine that you may have lost some of the initiative, zest, and drive that characterized you *before* you were married. Make a list of all those activities, hobbies, and interests that you may have given up when you married, and see what you can do about reviving them now. Look at your present period of living as a new beginning, a new start, a new challenge, not as the end of a marital career with the prospect of a lonely old age. Though you may often miss the comforts of your former married life, don't forget that these comforts also involved commitments and obligations of which you are free at present.

Consider moving to a new locality. Although moving away from the neighborhood where you lived while married may be inconvenient, it is, nevertheless, often worth the effort. This suggestion seems particularly appropriate if you lived in suburbia, or in a very small community that was essentially "married-couple-oriented," and thus provided few or no recreational or social outlets for the needs of the unmarried. There is actually no reason why you should live in and support a small community if, directly or indirectly, it discriminates against you because you are divorced. The opportunities for establishing a new circle of friends and for meeting people in situations similar to your own are often much better in a large urban community than in a small one. In general, I have found that the unmarried person is often less lonely in the supposedly cold and unfriendly environment of a large town than he is in a small town. Though it takes time and initiative to meet the right kind of friends in a metropolitan area, this effort will be worthwhile in the long run.

If you are a confirmed admirer of small-town life, it will be hard to convince you of the advantages a big city has to offer. However, if you are willing to consider moving to a metropolitan area, here are some of the advantages: First, as a divorcé you have more anonymity and much more freedom to come and go as you please. Generally, none of your neighbors know or care to know when you come home or don't come home, whom you date, and with what kind of people you associate. Thus, you don't have to be quite as concerned about your reputation. Second, just one look at the classified pages of the telephone directory in a large town is enough to make your vision blur from the large number of social clubs, groups, societies, bowling alleys, community activities, and adult education and recreation centers that you find listed there. Not that you necessarily want to join all these organizations, but you could participate in some of their activities if you wanted to. Finally, the person who is living in a more densely populated environment will find that a larger age range exists among the people whom he meets. You can have your choice of young, middle-aged, and older people; and more of them are "eligible" than in a small town.

You may have heard about the hustle and bustle of city life, the lack of fresh air, the crowded trains, buses, and subways and are therefore all prepared to dislike it. Also you have probably been told that people are less friendly in large towns. Notwithstanding all this, you may enjoy city life and find that it can offer many advantages to you as a divorce. Give it a try. You can always move back to a small community if you prefer it.

Try hard to be the right kind of father even though your divorced wife may have custody of your child or children. If the court has given your wife custody of the children, your previous daily contact with them may now be constricted to a few hours' or days' visit. When you visit your children it is most important *not* to spoil them in an attempt to make up for the many other times that you are unable to see them; for it is not so much what you give your children when you visit them (whether you take them to the most expensive shows or give them candy), but how much *real interest* you show in them that counts. During such visits avoid, too, (1) testing your children with too many ques-

117

tions about your previous wife's life just to satisfy your curiosity; (2) putting their mother into an unfavorable light; (3) forcing a high degree of confidence and intimacy with your children that may take a longer time to build up; (4) competing with your wife for their affection. You can be certain, however, that you will retain the love and respect of your children if you act natural and *relaxed* as a "visiting father."

Though you may be inclined to feel anxious about "losing" your children initially because you see so little of them, let me emphasize that what has already been established during the closeness of the early (and usually most formative and influential) years of development will persist despite the fact that you are with them less now. For suggested reading see footnote page 114.

Do not become a woman hater. If disappointment in your marriage has hurt you deeply, you could now easily become a cynic and misogynist, rejecting the whole female species because of your marriage failure. This does not mean, of course, that you stop paying attention to women, but it could mean that you stop taking them seriously, and refrain permanently from any involved and serious relationship with a woman. To react this way for a while is natural after a defeating and humiliating emotional experience. However, to *continue* to hold a grudge (based on generalization from *one* experience) seems neurotic and immature. For a while, your need for female love, understanding, and companionship may remain dormant, but this shouldn't be a reason to build a permanent protective wall around yourself. Such a barrier could keep you emotionally safe and protected now, but would make you increasingly lonely and dissatisfied as you grow older.

REMARRIAGE

Most divorces, after a period of recovery from the wounds inflicted by an unhappy marriage and divorce, are ready to make another try for matrimonial happiness. If this is your case, you will be glad to know that sociological statistics show second marriages to have an excellent chance for success (often this chance is better than that for first marriages).

If you are contemplating remarriage, I would like to offer the following suggestions:

Try to learn from your past mistakes. What was *really* wrong with your marriage? What were some of the reasons that led to it in the first place? The following is a list (compiled by marriage counselors) of some faulty reasons for marriage.

Desire for the status and prestige of marriage.

Infatuation mistaken for love.

Too much pressure from family and friends.

The desire for a mother or father-substitute.

The hope that marriage would change the undesirable personality traits of a spouse.

Under- or *over*rating the importance of sex in marriage.

Fear of loneliness.

To escape from home.

Fear of not finding someone better.

Inability to break off an undesirable love relationship.

These, then, are some of the *false* reasons for marriage and though a mild manifestation of a few of them do not always spell future disaster for a marriage relationship, *beware* if reasoning of the kinds described above is the main basis for a new entanglement.

Choose a new mate who is not too much like and yet not too different from the person whom you married before. Why we feel attracted so repeatedly to the same type of individual (though we often know that they are bad for us or could hurt us) is still a mystery to most people. Is it some unknown chemical attraction (a euphemistic term often used for sexual attraction)? Is it the unconscious image of a loved parent or of a childhood crush that we try to recapture in adulthood? Nobody

119

knows for certain, though the psychologists do think that unconscious childhood ideas and identifications probably trick us
into many relationships that our conscious selves later find hard
to grasp. However this may be, you must make certain *now* that
your second spouse does not turn out to be (in disguise or in a
slightly varied form) just as unsuitable for you as the first one.
You must try to prevent being the victim of what psychoanalysts
call a "repetition compulsion" (a forceful tendency to make the
same mistake repeatedly which operates in us all). Perhaps you
should make a list of those characteristics of your spouse to
which you were particularly allergic during your past marriage.
Then make doubly certain that you don't find the same or similar
sources of irritation in the person whom you now plan to marry.

However, in your attempt to compensate for what has
been amiss in your previous marriage, don't now go to the other
extreme and look for the kind of wife or husband whose personality is *completely opposite to that of your previous mate.* For
instance, if you are a man who has been married to an alcoholic,
your idea of the only eligible woman is one who won't touch a
drop of liquor. If you, as a woman, thought your husband was
too wrapped up in his work, you may now willingly settle down
only with someone who loathes the idea of any kind of work or
effort. The problems which we have had in past relationships
tend to make us oversensitive. It is important to guard against
this in the new social connections that we form with others.

Where to find eligible marital partners? I admit it may not
be quite as easy for you now that you have been burnt and are
perhaps a little older than the average person with whom you
are competing as a future marital partner. Though you may envy
your younger social competitors for their youth and attraction,
you can win if you give yourself a fair chance, and use your
greater maturity and experience to your advantage. Besides,
there are many people who feel that there is something highly
special and interesting about a divorcé. Though the premise

120

from which they draw this conclusion may not be valid, their bias nevertheless works to your advantage and often gives you a good start in establishing new and constructive relationships.

CHAPTER 13

Unwanted
Pregnancy

There are few problems that have been argued about more, have caused more heartache, and have yet remained more unsettled than that of the woman who is unmarried and has conceived without wanting to. Despite medical advances in the field of birth control, and despite a somewhat more tolerant and enlightened attitude on the part of the public, some of the emotional problems of an unwed mother or a woman facing an unwanted pregnancy, are not so very different today from what they were many years ago.

If, as the result of unwanted pregnancy, you find yourself anxious and tormented by inner conflicts, the following advice, mixing common sense judgment with psychological experience, is designed to help you.

Try to confide in someone; do not keep everything within yourself. This is very important. Though it is understandable that you may have the desire to keep things more secret than ever, you should find at least one individual in whom you can fully confide, and who can serve as a sounding board for what you want to do about your pregnancy. Besides, total repression of your problems is rarely possible. If you feel very apprehensive about something, it is bound to show up in your voice, your face, and your gestures. As a result, others may come to suspect the very thing that you are trying to hide from them.

Perhaps the best confidant in such a situation would be a professional individual who is not permitted to divulge information of this kind (such as a physician, psychiatrist, psychologist, or social worker). However, even confiding in a trusted and reliable friend whom you have known over a considerable period of time, would be better than keeping everything bottled up within yourself.

If you are emotionally close to both or either one of your parents, you may tell them about your pregnancy, but perhaps not before you are absolutely sure of it on the basis of medical tests and clinical evidence. Otherwise, you will create a family "storm" unnecessarily and prematurely. The fact that you have conceived without being married can be harder to confess than a crime. Nevertheless, others may be far more broad-minded and tolerant than you think, after the initial reaction of shock at your confession has worn off.

However, the time will come when the physical changes of pregnancy become obvious and you will find yourself being gazed at with curious and often calculating eyes by your friends, and should you be working, by your co-workers and supervisors. You may just as well prepare yourself for the highly personal and embarrassing questions that will be asked sooner or later. And it won't be easy to evade them with white lies or to blame your appearance on fatigue or obesity.

How much of the truth you can confess to others at this point will depend upon how close you are with your friends and co-workers. Your *real* friends will probably not like you less for letting them in on your secret. If more casual acquaintances begin to prod you with too many embarrassing questions, shrug them off with comments like these: "This is personal and I don't wish to tell you. Must I tell you *everything?*" Of course, you don't have to use these terms *verbatim* but should translate them into your own lingo.

If you are working, what you decide to reveal about your

present condition to your employer has a lot to do with your future plans. If your mind is set upon giving the child up for adoption, you could try to request a leave of absence from your job for reasons of health. Nobody need know what really happened when you return to work. If, on the other hand, you want to keep your child and, at the same time, continue to work as long as your physical condition will permit, it may be wisest to reveal the truth, since you will eventually have to.

Do not believe that your pregnancy will make it impossible to continue your work. Much, of course, depends upon the amount of *physical* strain involved on your job. If you are working in an office or hold a position that does not require excess physical exertion, there is no reason for you to quit immediately. In fact, continuing to work for a while could be good for you from a mental health point of view. It could keep you occupied and thus prevent you from worrying unnecessarily about your physical condition, yourself, and your future.

Should you get fired as a result of your present condition, it would be advisable for you to contact some of the social agencies to be mentioned in more detail at the end of this chapter.

Do not hate or punish yourself for what has happened. Though you may worry about what your family, your friends, and others may think, your most excruciating problem may well be *what you think of yourself* and what all this has done to your own self-respect.

In trying to ease the anxiety of your present state, you must not allow yourself to be upset by the many movies and novels that create a highly dramatized and negative, but not always realistic, image of the unwed, pregnant woman. Your tendency to blame yourself excessively and to be overanxious, may stem from what you have read and what, as the result of it, you fantasize and anticipate. More dangerously, an unconscious need to punish yourself could express itself by enhanced accident-proneness, a general devil-may-care attitude that makes you cross the streets against the lights, or causes you to drive your car more recklessly. Though your unconscious may push you strongly toward such action, you must fight these tendencies by realizing that indulging the impulse toward self-destruction will leave you worse off than you were before. Difficult as it may be, you must learn to live with yourself by adapting to your present situation. Though you may dislike the physical state you are in, you must not reject yourself as a person.

Decide clearly and definitely what you want to do *about your pregnancy.* Have you thought about an abortion? Do not be afraid of admitting such a thought to yourself. This does not mean that you are necessarily lacking in motherly feeling or have murderous tendencies. It could be that you resent only the conditions under which you became pregnant, not the whole concept and idea of motherhood.

Firstly, an abortion is an illegal act, and giving one's consent to it or participating in it involves guilt and anxiety. Even individuals whose social consciences are underdeveloped are bound to suffer when they engage in activities that are not approved by the society in which they live. Secondly, even wealthy or affluent people find it difficult if not impossible to convince a properly qualified physician to risk losing his license and reputation in order to perform the wanted operation.

Finding it difficult to obtain an abortion in the United States, perhaps you have considered traveling to a foreign country where different laws prevail. The ease with which abortions can be obtained on foreign soil has, however, often been somewhat exaggerated. Even though the attitudes of some European and Oriental nations are different from our own with regard to abortion, these countries, too, have medical and hospital groups who decide under what circumstances an abortion is feasible. If you are over 3 months pregnant even Europe or Japan is not the Utopia for pregnant women that many expectant mothers think.

However, some established facts are: almost all women who have had an abortion performed agree that it has constituted some kind of psychological trauma. Some have had postoperative complications. Usually very anxious women who have always been hypersensitive to pain have the greatest difficulties with abortions. It goes without saying that the greatest number of accidents and complications occurred in illegal abortions performed under unsanitary conditions.

Consider this too: though relief from the anxiety of your pregnancy might be worth almost any price or risk, you may not feel the same way *after* an abortion has been performed. You may have strong unconscious desires to keep the child, which are repressed at present. After an abortion has been performed these latent desires may be released and plague you with strong feelings of guilt and regret.

In your present crisis you may have thought of obtaining an abortion for psychiatric reasons. But this is usually not as easy as you may think. The fact that you are quickly upset (particularly now), or at times suffer depression, would by no means suffice for a psychiatrist to certify that your state of sanity could be endangered through the act of childbirth. Only under circumstances in which severe mental or emotional derangement are present would such a medical recommendation be given.

In view of all these circumstances it may be better for you not to consider abortion; instead, if you absolutely don't want the child, give it up for adoption later on. If you do decide *not* to seek an abortion, problems about the future course of your life in relation to your pregnancy are not always over at this point. The expected child's father may not be willing to marry you, even though you want him to. In fact, he might even pressure you to seek an abortion. You may be suddenly confused, and your feelings about the man jumbled. Or, should marriage be contemplated, you hesitate to marry someone with whom you are not really in love. Each one of these dilemmas could create a major conflict in you, the resolution of which requires emotional wisdom and foresight.

To definitely advise anybody in these matters without knowing all the individual circumstances and the people involved would be presumptuous. If you are in this predicament, however, and are searching for a few principles to guide you in making the right decision, the following might be applicable:

Since you cannot always be one hundred per cent sure how much you love the man whom you marry, or of his feelings for you, it would certainly be taking a grave risk to speak the marriage vows just because of your pregnancy. There are many loveless marriages that take place because a child is on the way, but many of these marriages end in divorce and work to the ultimate disadvantage of the child.

A case in point is that of Ruth J., a ballet dancer who during her second month of pregnancy married a young man whom she had met only about half a year before but did not love. Though Ruth's own judgment told her that it was wrong to marry this man, she finally gave in to family pressures, and saved her reputation by agreeing to a quick marriage. She is divorced now, finds it difficult to remarry, and her son has turned out to be a juvenile delinquent. She wishes now that she had not married at the time she was pregnant. There are many other cases of this kind in the records of social service agencies.

If your pregnancy has made you hate the man whom you thought you cared for, and if these feelings persist, it would be inadvisable to marry him. It is of course true that no love relationship is ever entirely free from temporary irritation, disappointment, and anger. However, if such attitudes persist and outweigh the more positive feelings, the odds are heavily set against a good future marriage relationship.

To be a mother without a husband and to raise a child without a father may not be as impossible as you think. I am fully aware of the serious problems involved in this situation. Nevertheless, sometimes to have *no husband* or *no father for your child* is better than to be under the influence of a man who is very immature and unstable, and with whom you are incompatible to the extent that marriage and family life are destroyed. Though you may shudder at the thought of leading the life of an unwed mother, remember that such a life does not preclude the chance of marrying someone else in the future who is compatible with you and with whom you are genuinely in love. There are many instances where this has happened. It is also possible to create a healthy psychological environment for a fatherless child, though it is, of course, more difficult than under ordinary circumstances. You may be helped in your effort to do this by learning from the experiences of other single parents and by being able to share some of your problems with them. An organization that calls itself "Parents Without Partners," and which plans many social, recreational, and educational events for the single parent, may be of help to you in this connection. The organization's main office is in New York City, at 80 Fifth Avenue, and the telephone number is CHelsea 3-3060. There are branches of this organization in other cities and communities.

Find the right sources for help. In your desperate desire for help, you may turn in many different directions and, feeling confused, you may think that *any* advice coming from someone else is better than your own. However, you must realize that only you yourself can ultimately make the right decisions, and the people who can best help you are psychiatrists, psychologists, and social workers, who have had experience in dealing with problems that are similar to yours.

Most of the agencies that specialize in counseling work with unwed mothers are located in the larger cities. You will find them listed in the classified telephone directory under Social

Service Organizations. However, if you live in a smaller community, write or call the agencies in the larger cities and they will make the appropriate referral to sources in your own area.

Since I practice therapy in New York City, I am most familiar with the local New York social services for unmarried mothers. Most of these agencies offer services which include financial and medical assistance, help in finding suitable employment, and legal advice. They will leave it up to you to decide whether you want to keep the child or make plans for future adoption. The names and telephone numbers of some of the agencies in New York City are:

Inwood House
223 West 15th Street
New York, New York 10011
WAtkins 9-4960
Casework service for unmarried mothers with psychological and psychiatric consultation. Medical care, maternity residence and foster home care.

Catholic Charities of the Archdiocese of New York City
122 East 22nd Street
New York, New York 10010
ORegon 7-5000
Program includes prenatal and postnatal shelter care, placement plan for infants, and future planning for and rehabilitation of mother.

Louise Wise Services
10-12 East 94th Street
New York, New York 10028
TRafalgar 6-3050
Casework service for Jewish unmarried mothers.

Lutheran Child Welfare Association
422 West 44th Street
New York, New York 10036
CIrcle 5-6500

Casework counseling, shelter care planning, temporary boarding care, and adoption homes provided for Protestant (primarily Lutheran) unwed mothers.

CHAPTER **14** / Facing Life
Alone

For a variety of reasons, many people find themselves suddenly faced with the prospect of living alone; the single man or woman who has moved into a new locality; the recently widowed, divorced or separated individual; or the aging person who has been precipitantly thrown upon his own resources. Whatever the circumstances, if you are newly living alone, you probably have already discovered that single life presents a difficult adjustment. Certain long-term and other more immediate problems call upon you to revise many of your previous habits and attitudes. Coping with loneliness, emptiness, and depression, the everpresent pitfalls of a single life, will utilize all of your emotional wisdom and maturity. It is to help you make the most of these qualities in yourself that the following suggestions are offered. These guide-points are really not meant as final solutions (since there are as many solutions as there are individuals), but are presented more in the spirit of first aid, as certain over-all aids do exist which apply to everyone who is learning to live alone.

Don't be embarrassed by your status as a single person. Although, statistically speaking, the majority of the population is paired off, this does not make you a social oddity. Besides, others are usually far too occupied with their own worries to care about the impression you make as a single person.

There has never been a time when the unmarried person has been accepted with less prejudice than today. The old notion that divorcées, spinsters or bachelors have to be queer or abnormal because they live alone has almost been abandoned in modern society. Many psychologists and sociologists would agree that marriage is only one way of living, that a single life can often be equally productive and meaningful.

Don't be afraid of being single. Though you may be firmly convinced that you never can or will marry or remarry, circumstances may arise that could make you change your mind. Furthermore, don't let the prospect of a lonely future frighten you. Your life will only be as lonely *as you want it to be.* History abounds with examples of unmarried people who have lived productive, satisfactory, and useful lives without a basic feeling of being alone.

Don't feel sorry for yourself. Avoid self-pity and false sentimentalization of your present condition. It is so easy to adopt a "poor lonely me" attitude and to wallow in it. Too much affection spent on yourself merely drains off emotional energy that could be directed toward others. Only helpless infants feel that the world has come to an end because they are temporarily left alone. You as an adult have the resources and powers to cope with this situation. Try to bear your loneliness with pride and strength and others will respect you for it.

Realize that along with the difficulties of a single life, there are some advantages: you have more freedom and independence, it costs less to live alone, and you don't have to account to anybody for your actions. Think for a moment of the many husbands, wives, and parents who, caught in a tight web of social pressure and commitment, often envy you for your relative freedom and independence and the fact that you are not held to a rigid schedule—just as you as a lonely person, may envy their social situations.

Your period of living alone can help you to develop new

hobbies, interests, and skills, and may be the time for you to discover yourself. Though your personality make-up is probably not that of a monk or hermit (who *voluntarily* seek solitude), you can gain many valuable insights about yourself by living alone for a while. For if you can manage to adjust to your own moods and idiosyncrasies as a single person, you will find it much easier to adapt to those of others.

Learn to enjoy the pleasure of observation. As a single person, conditions may arise in which you must engage alone in many activities which others usually share. You may be forced into the role of a spectator when you really want to be a participant. But why worry about it and pity yourself? Instead, view your solitude as an unusual opportunity to sharpen your powers of perception of the outside world. The feeling of inner emptiness that makes loneliness so unpleasant is often caused by too much introspection and excess preoccupation with yourself. Try to counteract it by becoming more extraverted. Now is the time to become more keenly aware of the buildings, flowers, animals, and, of course, people that surround you and to pay the attention to them that would be difficult were you preoccupied with someone else's company. For instance, when dining out alone, you can have a most interesting time observing the other patrons. Try looking at the world for a while through the eyes of the writer, poet, or painter. Though you are alone, your loneliness will lose its unpleasant sting. (It is probably significant that creative individuals voluntarily *seek* solitude to sharpen and widen their range of experience.) The imaginative and observant individual has no time to feel lonely and deserted.

Anticipate lonely hours and days and try to fill them with some kind of activity ahead of time. The single adult must plan his or her free time more carefully than the family member who has part of his social life at home. Though unexpected visits and surprise calls can often brighten your lonely evenings or weekends, you can never completely depend upon such chance happenings. If, as a single person, you are afraid of loneliness, you are the one who must take the initiative, organize your time, and use every bit of your foresight and imagination to forestall future empty hours.

A life with definite future plans and worthwhile goals is seldom lonely. Experience seems to suggest that the single man or woman is particularly prone to spells of loneliness on Sunday mornings, Saturday nights, during holidays, and during the early evening hours. Perhaps these are times that we have learned to associate with social activity in the past and that is why it especially bothers us when we find ourselves alone during these hours or days. To combat such feelings before they overpower you, it is therefore essential to plan some kind of meaningful activity *in advance* for those hours during which you expect to be most vulnerable to the ache of loneliness. Such activity does not always have to involve other people. Reading your favorite book or magazine, attending a movie, or buying a small gift for yourself or others may be the "pill" that relieves loneliness and depression.

If you can't think of anything worthwhile to do in your spare time, blame only your own lack of imagination and resourcefulness. It may be no fun to go to the movies by yourself, to taste foreign dishes in a restaurant without someone else to relish them with you, or to be unable to share the beauty of paintings at a museum with another person. But isn't it better than to sit by yourself at home or to walk around aimlessly in the streets? Besides, any enterprise that you start planning by yourself could open the door to new contacts or friendships (people have met in the strangest places).

This does not imply, of course, that you have to be frantically busy every minute of your time. There may be occasions when you welcome the idea of being alone and enjoy it. Only if loneliness bothers you is it necessary to take precautions ahead of time.

Your home should include a radio or TV set, many good

books, and a telephone. A radio or TV set is there to break the silence of the single person's living quarters. Though you may welcome the hush of your apartment many times, continuous quiet can enhance a sense of loneliness. Switch on the news or a program you enjoy to keep in touch with the outside world and it will distract you from excess preoccupation with yourself. A background of radio music can do much to lift lonely spirits.

It is often stated that "books are a man's best friend." Though this is an exaggerated statement, there is some truth in it, especially when circumstances render it hard, for a while, to find those friends and affiliations which are truly satisfactory. Obviously, the adventures encountered in novels and stories are only a feeble substitute for the presence of real experiences and people. However, in many instances the right kind of book can help enrich a lonely weekend or an empty evening.

For many people the habit of reading is not a natural one, and may take some time to develop, but it is a worthwhile pastime to cultivate, particularly if circumstances force you to live by yourself. To really enjoy reading, free yourself from the idea that you *must* read certain books that are acclaimed by the public or recommended by others. Attempt to make your own friends among the authors, without regard for the taste of others. Go to the literature that enthralls you, distracts you, or gives you some kind of solace and reassurance.

Though a telephone can be a nuisance sometimes, it can also be a most valuable bridge to the outside world for the single man or woman. You may want to build up a small and carefully selected circle of telephone friends and acquaintances, whom you can call when you feel the need to talk and to express yourself. Sometimes discussing the most trivial events or occurrences can dispel the onset of a lonely mood. Though you will be billed for every minute of your conversation at the end of the month, it will be money well spent if it eliminates the feeling of being out of touch with others.

Try to meet people on your own instead of depending ex-

clusively upon your friends' friends. Married couples and family friends will continually want to introduce you to others or try to play cupid. Though you should not turn down such social opportunities, don't be too disappointed if they often fail to live up to your expectations. Apparently the best and most enjoyable relationships are those which we choose ourselves, not those that have been chosen for us by others. Our own emotional and social intuition seems to fulfill our needs most adequately.

In your search for affiliation with others, avoid the mistake of joining just any social group in order to get away from the confinement of being by yourself. Be very selective and discriminating about joining clubs and organizations that have been formed primarily for the purpose of bringing lonely or single people together. Although some worthwhile people can be found in such clubs, a large number of members may have joined because of personality difficulties of their own which make them poor companions for you. Also, meeting people in clubs and organizations about which you have little knowledge may serve to make you more lonely for those you have known previously in your life who have meant more to you.

If you decide to join a social organization, it should probably be one that stresses activity, instead of "aloneness," a club to which you can bring a skill or talent for which you may be appreciated. Do you write poetry? A writer's organization would be best for you. Are you interested in politics and current events? Then don't join the local charity chapter, or the hospital volunteer corps to "meet people," but instead become a member of a political organization.

Of course, seeking group or club affiliation is only one of the ways of finding relief from loneliness, and it may not be your way. Perhaps you are the kind of person who thrives much better in the friendship of only one or two people whom you meet occasionally and who are meaningful to you. If you really believe this, you should avoid joining groups. Though this may mean that you have to hold out over a longer period of time till you find the right kind of friendship and affiliation, it is worthwhile for you to do so.

Make wise use of the extra free time that you often have as a single person. The fact that you are not occupied with the problems of marriage or family life could afford you an unusual opportunity to further your education and knowledge, to develop new hobbies and interests.

These then, are the positive ways to enrich your life as a single person. Naturally, it is better to concentrate on the ways of imparting affirmative meaning and joy to your existence but, to do so effectively, you must be aware of negative behavior and thought patterns that might entrap you. The following case histories illustrate dangerous means of escaping loneliness—means to be avoided, as they usually only aggravate the condition.

ESCAPE INTO OVERWORK

A lonely bachelor accountant whom I know spent almost all his weekends and holidays working in his office to combat solitude. As a result, he had very little social life, and developed an increasing feeling of isolation which eventually led to a severe depression and a nervous breakdown.

Another case in point is that of a female business executive, who, to get over the hump the weekend represented, took a job as a waitress Saturdays and Sundays. The accumulated and constant strain of a high-pressure job and the physical demands of waitressing combined to give her a stomach ulcer.

While a certain amount of work does serve to bring you out of yourself, to give you an interest, and to occupy your time, overdoing it leads to an unpleasant end.

ESCAPE INTO LIQUOR

A popular form of escaping loneliness is to attempt to wash it away in alcohol. For the person who feels socially deprived and lonely, the bottle can easily become the best and most readily available friend. With a glass in hand, the lonely hours speed by and the need for company becomes less acute and painful.

Mrs. R. B. is an example of how unsuccessful this method of escape can be. An attractive woman in her fifties, Mrs. B. is married to a prominent lawyer. Her husband, being a busy man, does not have much time for her during the day. Her son is grown and married. She found herself increasingly spending time alone. During this lonely time, she became the victim of spells of depression and, though she had many friends and there were numerous activities she might undertake, she succumbed to a compulsion to sit in her room and brood. In this state, she discovered that alcohol could give her a feeling of warmth and contentment that made her *enjoy* her loneliness. She could only attain this feeling while drinking by herself, never in company. Her yearning for these lonely hours of drinking became so intense that she began to turn down all social engagements and withdrew more and more into herself. In trying to escape her loneliness, she trapped herself into an even deeper isolation, and estranged herself from her family and friends.

ESCAPE INTO SEX AND SOCIAL LIFE

Other lonely men and women find relief from the dull throb of solitude by engaging in an intense hunt for love and sex which takes their minds off themselves and provides them with a goal. Resort hotels, bars, and lonely-hearts clubs are filled with people who pretend to seek companionship and "good, clean fun" but who hope basically that sex or love will provide the cure for their state of isolation.

The case histories of Valery and Herman are helpful in demonstrating how the search to end loneliness through sex can wind up in despair and frustration.

Valery, an attractive woman in her thirties, is a typical social butterfly. Never at a loss for words, adept with people, she goes out constantly, fearing the attacks of loneliness that invariably possess her whenever, rarely, she has an evening alone. Even in the midst of company, she finds herself prone to spells of depression and feelings of alienation which she covers up with bright talk. She attributes her condition to her loveless and unmarried state. Thinking she simply has not found the right man for her, she goes from one to another in an unceasing and frantic search for the perfect husband, yet none will do. Each brief encounter leaves her feeling more than ever alone. Driven by her inner loneliness and hunger for love and affection, she suffers from a compulsion never to miss a party, never to miss a date. And yet her frenetic struggles to escape her lonely self cannot yield the assuagement she seeks.

* * *

Pietje, who also thought that his main source of despair was loneliness, experienced solitude in a different way. An immigrant from Holland, he sought, like Valery, to mitigate his loneliness by joining social clubs, but unlike her he gave them up as they did not meet with his approval. He took to frequenting bars and public dances in an attempt to escape the confining loneliness of his room, and at one of these he met Theresa. They became friends, and at first, basking in her admiration, he found relief from inner emptiness through the excitement of

139

sexual intercourse. However, the honeymoon was soon over, and Pietje began being extremely hostile and critical toward his new companion, complaining that she was boring and lacking in social refinement. He began to long for the days when he was unattached and uncommitted to anyone. However, when Theresa finally left him, he was extremely unhappy and miserably aware of his state of social isolation. Finally, hopelessly depressed by his loneliness, he was found in his dingy furnished room close to death from an overdose of sleeping pills.

By *using* other people as a *means* to end loneliness, by perceiving others only as they pertained to themselves and not as independent individuals, Valery and Herman locked themselves further into solitude. By not genuinely reaching *out* to others the self remains alone.

PART THREE

Troubled

Relationships

CHAPTER 15

Estrangement
in Marriage

Visit a photographer who specializes in wedding pictures. Look at the snapshots displayed and pay special attention to the gleam of affection and love in the faces of the newlyweds. If pictures of the same couples were taken again twenty, thirty, or forty years after the wedding date, how many shots would still show the same expressions of care and interest? Perhaps only a few. In fact, some of the couples would probably be divorced after all that time.

The question arises then: what is it that makes so many marriages falter and fail? Are there prophetic signs or symptoms that point to failure, and if so, could their early detection save some these unions? I believe so; therefore, let me give you some of these early and often quite unconscious manifestations of marriage trouble which have come to my attention as a therapist.

BREAKDOWN IN COMMUNICATION

One of the main symptoms is a breakdown in communication. In plain English this means a fear or inhibition to express freely to wife or husband what is on your mind. Long barren islands of silence arise suddenly in the stream of conversation, where formerly there was a ready and spontaneous flow of words. Suddenly it is no longer possible for you to talk and to confide. Furthermore, when you speak with him or her, your thoughts tend to wander; you have lost the real interest to listen and to care. Psychoanalysts state that sometimes it is not what the patient verbalizes in therapy but what he does *not* verbalize which is significant—the long silences and omissions. I believe the same holds true sometimes in marital relationships, and I regard therefore the beginning of lack of communication between two people one of the most serious indicators that there is something wrong with the marital relationship.

INAPPROPRIATE TEMPER OUTBURSTS

Fits of fury that cannot be accounted for by outside tensions stemming from work or other sources are often danger signals. If your wife flies off the handle because you forget to put back the toothpaste cap, or if your husband suddenly throws a fit because you are two minutes late for an appointment, there is a good possibility that at least a few subconscious forces of hostility are at work undermining your marital relationship. While these forces are still weak and not too well established, you may be able to control them. It is never too *early* to try to counteract them.

FORGETFULNESS

The sudden forgetting of special dates (such as a birthday or wedding anniversary), or forgetting the things that you know your wife or husband might like (buying the wrong presents), arouses suspicion that your marriage is not quite as good as it was at the start. Psychoanalysts have found that forgetting is rarely incidental. Naturally, the appointment or date that has been overlooked is not one that we were too eager about. It is for this reason that so many unpleasant bills remain neglected and unpaid for a long time. Nobody has ever been known to forget to collect a thousand-dollar check. That brides and bridegrooms have been known to forget their wedding day does not

144

contradict this theory in view of the last-minute uncertainties some people experience about marriage.

EXCESS MOODINESS

Excess moodiness, which could also be due to a number of other extramarital factors (business problems, physiological causes), may nevertheless be a foreboding signal that not all is well in your marriage. Thus, the wife or husband who acts depressed wants to convey in an indirect manner: "Don't you see how miserable I am? But I'm ashamed to say it out loud. *Do* something!" It would probably be more natural and constructive for one to come right out and say these things but to some extent, we are all cowards at heart.

At other times depressions can mean the experience of guilt and self-condemnation, perhaps because of inability to fulfill marital demands or infidelity in the relationship. Regardless of the causes, severe and lasting depressions can be like the rumbling of volcanoes which forecast that there is something wrong on the inside that could erupt at some future time.

SEXUAL SYMPTOMS

Other marital difficulties make their first appearance in the form of a *disturbance of the sex life.* If there is sudden coldness in sex, where there was love, warmth, and receptivity before, and if this attitude continues over a long period of time, this may be a sign of unconscious hostility in the marital relationship. This is particularly true in the case of women, who often respond more slowly than men, especially when they feel emotionally hurt or resentful. In the case of men, a basic marital resentment or a cooling off can express itself sexually not only by lack of ardor and passion, but also by lack of patience, consideration, and tenderness.

All these small or large signs of irritation may be the first steps in a long trail that could lead from slight dissatisfaction to strong resentment, and sometimes to separation and divorce. What, then, are the countermeasures to be taken now, while your marriage is ailing, but is not yet sick enough to be terminated?

Have a certain amount of blind faith in the future of your marriage. If your marriage is not too disturbed and the problems not too great, you must believe in its future and be willing to take some chances on it. It is easy to do this as long as everything is going smoothly. However, the strength of your faith is not really tested or challenged *until a crisis occurs.* You should exhaust every other possibility before you consider divorce or separation, which sometimes represent escape rather than a solution. If you obtain a divorce prematurely, feelings of guilt, remorse, and regret may become so intense in your future as a divorcé that they could make you even more unhappy. A renewed faith and confidence—even if unfounded—may be the medicine that your marriage needs most to revive it.

Don't take your marriage for granted. Don't assume that you are happily married simply because your wife or husband does not complain. As was mentioned before, sudden spells of silence and pseudo-quietness in a marriage can sometimes project a false sense of security and can be more dangerous than raised fists or violent arguments. Therefore, do not hesitate to break the silent deadlock that can so often exist between two people who are in love by uttering such blunt statements as these: "What is wrong with our relationship? We can't talk to each other any more. Is there something bothering you?" Comments of this kind, voiced at the right moment, and with tact, may reveal the causes of marital difficulties and problems before they have had a chance to gather momentum in the repressed and unconscious part of the personality. You may risk a rebuff, a cold shoulder, or the accusation of being a nagging wife or husband by asking such questions, but this is a small price to pay for keeping the marital lines of communication open.

The delicate fibers of the marital ties need periodic testing to assure their durability and strength. Many divorced couples have later attributed their unhappiness to the fact that they did not speak of their difficulties to each other. Therefore, as a precautionary measure, become perceptive to the language of silence.

Change some long established routines. This may be the shot of adrenalin (figuratively speaking) that your marriage needs to be put on its feet. A common factor in marital dissatisfaction is too much routine. Many wives would prefer a husband who deviates from the established routine to one who is as predictable as a Swiss cuckoo clock. Though some people go to the other extreme and are too unpredictable, it is nevertheless the routines and chores of marriage that often kill the romance and glow which were present at first.

Most people realize the need for a change in their daily chores, but they are too slow to understand the need to alter the habits of love and sex occasionally. Perhaps insecurity or ancient prejudice make people rigid and unimaginative when it comes to the more intimate aspects of love in married life. Many marriages have deteriorated not because of infidelity and incompatibility but because of sheer boredom and what may be called "routine-itis." Make sure, therefore, that *your* marriage is not atrophying for this reason.

"Fight it out" if you must, but do it in a fair manner. Though marital fights and arguments can take a lot of energy out of you, they seem to be necessary, at times, to clear the air and to release pent-up tensions, at least for some couples. There are two main reasons for the frequency of fights in some marriages: the need for artificial excitement in an otherwise too calm relationship, and the prospect of reconciliation. Whatever the reasons, if you *must* fight in order to keep your marriage on an even keel, try to do your fighting at least in a *fair* manner.

Perhaps you should try to draw up a written peace treaty

during the more calm periods of your marriage with guarantees that in the future, when a war is declared between you, you will carry on some of your household chores, not bring in outsiders to support your arguments, and not continue your fights over forty-eight hours.

Don't overdo "togetherness." Though its importance has been strongly impressed upon married couples, an overdose of being together with *anybody* can become monotonous rather than pleasurable. It is natural and highly desirable, therefore, for couples not to cling to one another *all* the time and to retain their individuality as well as some of their individual hobbies and interests. Perhaps a little distance and separateness is what you, too, need to put your marriage on a new footing.

Do not hesitate to seek marital counseling or psychiatric advice if your problems have become severe. Marriage counseling is done by social workers, psychiatrists, psychologists, ministers, priests, and rabbis. The need for some kind of professional help is indicated whenever difficulties get out of hand or when divorce seems a serious possibility. Although many people with marital difficulties blame it all on conditions and circumstances (money, liquor, too much work, in-laws, living quarters), the experience of marriage consultants seems to suggest that *inner attitudes, feelings and complexes* are more often at the root of nuptial problems. These can be changed through professional help. It is not true that professional marriage counselors will necessarily either try to preserve the existing marriage at any cost or encourage divorce. Instead, they will recommend what is best under the circumstances. Sometimes this may mean divorce, at other times continuation of the marriage.

Much has been said about the unreliability of some marriage counselors who are not properly qualified. Perhaps it would be best for you to search for professional help by approaching a social work organization, or, if you are religiously inclined, contacting someone connected with your church or synagogue. As is mentioned in other parts of this book, the names of social work agencies are listed in classified telephone books under the heading of Social Service Organization. Information about professional services of this kind can also be obtained by writing to the administration and information division of the Community Service Society of New York (105 East 22nd Street, New York, New York, 10010, telephone, ALgonquin 4-8900). The individuals consulted are then likely to make further referrals if your situation warrants medical or psychiatric attention. If your marriage is in very serious danger it is, of course, of utmost importance that you seek professional help; in the beginning, it does not matter from what source. Hoping that things will eventually straighten themselves out is as irresponsible as failing to call a physician at the onset of a serious disease.

CHAPTER **16** / Fear of
Promiscuity

Persistent feelings of guilt, exhaustion, vague feelings of discomfort about being "different," and fears of being blackmailed cause people to consult psychotherapists because of their promiscuous tendencies. Such patients want to find a cure for what is referred to as adultery, polygamy, nymphomania, or satyriasis in its extreme forms.

What kind of people are these patients and what causes their behavior? First, there are those individuals who are promiscuous in fantasy only. Whenever an attractive woman enters the scene they undress her in their imagination. Such men (if they are married) commit mental adultery many times, but they are actually not dangerous. Although they always seem to wish for those women whom they cannot have, their affliction is relatively harmless since fear and lack of confidence makes them rarely carry out their sexual desires. Often their need to "look" and to take in imagination what they can't get in reality represents a regression to an earlier phase of sexual development.

Second, there are Casanova-like men. I call all of these "Casanovas" because they follow a pattern that was set down by the well-known Italian gentleman of this name. The psychology of the Casanova type of man is based on a morbid need to prove his masculinity. He is afraid of a single and lasting relationship because it may reveal his inadequacies or his basic shallowness of feeling. When so-called Casanovas marry, they do it primarily for reasons of prestige but continue just the same to seek new female conquests.

Bachelor Casanova types often lead highly promiscuous lives because they think there is safety in the number of women whom they know. They protect themselves from possible hurt by remaining free of long-term commitments, or by courting several women at the same time. Though essentially they follow the pleasure principle, their belief that close and lasting love must result in hurt and injury seems overly pessimistic. If unmarried Casanovas seek psychotherapy, it is usually because their pride has been hurt in one of their relationships with women, and it is then that they are beginning to doubt the wisdom of their hedonistic approach to life.

It is significant that no equally famous female replica of Casanova seems to have existed in history; however, I do believe that there are women who are Casanova-like in that they seek constant sexual change and excitement. Their basic insecurity makes them want to prove their femininity in terms of many rather than one man. When female Casanovas are married and carry on numerous extramarital affairs it is again because their way of seeking safety is a repeated flight into sex with different men. Though all women need male assurance, most of them can sublimate it in the form of occasional flirtation, and find satisfaction in the pleasure derived from men's compliments. A compliment, then, is symbolically a kiss through a veil.

A third group of people who are likely to be promiscuous are *chronic heartbreakers*. Such individuals often gain a morbid sense of satisfaction from hurting others because this "accomplishment" gives them a false sense of power and superiority. Their reasoning is: I may be the one who will eventually get hurt in this relationship and I couldn't bear such humiliation. Therefore I would rather be the one who inflicts the pain. Individuals who are given by such motives are constantly on the look-out for

151

new affairs, as they quickly lose interest in a relationship once their basically vindictive impulses have been satisfied.

Finally, there are, of course, many instances where physiological factors create a desire for continuous sexual release. In many cases, however, it has been found that psychological rather than physiological causes are responsible for inability to satiate the sex drive.

Some psychoanalysts believe that promiscuity is almost always a defense measure against latent homosexuality. The man who is driven so strongly to prove his masculinity must, according to this theory, defend himself against his unconscious desires or love for someone of the same sex. Whether one subscribes to this point of view would depend upon the acceptance of the Freudian school of psychoanalysis and its implications.

What can you do if you are aware of these and other promiscuous tendencies in yourself but can't control them?

Realize that there is pain as well as pleasure in promiscuity. To have an affair with every attractive person whom you see can seem a wonderful dream, but one that may burst like a bubble should it come true. What you yearn for in fantasy is rarely quite as beautiful in reality. Thus, the luscious woman whom you dream of conquering may reject you completely. The man who seems so masculine and strong may be impotent or lose his powers of attraction as you get to know him. So, actually, it may often be more rewarding to enjoy some of your sexual desires in imagination than in the harsh light of reality.

If you carry on several love affairs simultaneously, you will create much unpleasant tension and anxiety. I am reminded of the bachelor who had a date with a different woman almost every other night of the week. He had to shift his attention and his energies as rapidly as a harassed worker who holds several high-pressure part-time jobs. This made a nervous wreck of him, and when he came to consult me professionally, he asked for tranquilizing as well as energizing drugs to keep himself going.

He also suffered fresh attacks from his previously cured stomach ulcer. Though he *thought* he lived life to the fullest extent, he really felt emotionally exhausted and unhappy most of the time.

As a woman you may find it difficult to have many and often meaningless love affairs without a *lowering of your own self-esteem*. By living promiscuously, you may eventually feel like cheap merchandise that passes through many dirty hands when you actually want to feel like a precious jewel that has been selected because of its special value. Though we sometimes use others to satisfy our own needs, we are thus depriving ourselves of the beauty and enjoyment of a relationship by making it impersonal and arbitrary. One of the most satisfying pleasures of a love relationship is that it can enhance your femininity. Though you may also gain this sense of satisfaction by being desired by *many* and not only one member of the opposite sex, it can rarely compensate for the feeling of self-esteem that arises from the admiration, love, and care of *one* individual. It is a fact that promiscuous men and women often feel inferior about themselves. They cannot free themselves of the idea that there is something wrong with them. On the other hand, one satisfying love relationship does more to enhance your self-esteem and your sense of sexual identity than any number of affairs.

Should your life consist of a *succession of quick love affairs* that you plan to terminate as soon as they get more serious, you should try to realize this: breaking off an intimate relationship always involves pain and agony. Also, your sexual involvement may have made you more dependent upon your lover than you originally intended. A succession of such painful breakups can test your emotional equilibrium more severely than you think.

Suppose you don't get hurt? Let us assume that you are a cold and detached person who can't be hurt easily. Unconsciously, you may have learned how to build up defenses against deeper emotional involvement and its consequences. But even then you may find if difficult to cope with the feelings of *guilt*

153

that seize your conscience *after* you have broken off an affair. Could you remain completely unmoved if you were exposed to broken marriages, suicide attempts, tears, accusations, or the feeling within yourself that you have destroyed or injured another person's emotional life? It is, of course, true that there are some love and sex relationships that can be resolved pleasantly and without hurt or guilt on either side for the man or woman who is involved. But how often does this happen? Experience seems to indicate that it is very rare.

In promiscuity you may gain sexual satisfaction but dull your capacity to love. Although the need for sexual satisfaction is always present, most indivduals find it extremely difficult to be happy with only the fulfillment of sexual needs. We all need at least some love and affection. As a therapist I have found that patients' incapacity to give or receive love worries them more than their sexual problems.

All this is not meant to imply, of course, that a number of sexual affairs could deprive you *completely* of your future potential for love. Though there are some people who maintain that you get more wise and experienced with every new sexual relationship, it is also a fact that there is a limit to how much you can expend yourself emotionally. There must eventually be a point of depletion. It is almost a psychological *law* that anything done to an extreme and too repeatedly loses some of its attraction and thrill. Love, as well as sex, are like drinks which become tasteless if gulped down quickly and carelessly without appreciation of their unique flavor. Who has such an unlimited reservoir of love, sexual drive, and affection that he can keep on using it without reaching a point of depletion?

A life that is too full of excitement becomes exhausting because continually stronger stimuli are needed to enhance the pleasure. Too much excitement dulls the palate for pleasure. What holds true for our senses and appetites also applies to our sexual drives and needs. Trying for ever greater kicks in your so-called love relationships can therefore lead to a point of diminishing returns, or to ultimate perversion, despair, or repeated boredom and emptiness.

The promiscuous man or woman is like the child who nibbles food from an endless number of dishes and yet remains hungry and unsatisfied after all of them have been consumed. To satisfy fully your sexual appetite takes self-discipline and self-control, even though the idea of discipline seems almost opposed to pleasure. Many joys in life are enhanced and prolonged if they are controlled and held in abeyance at times by the capacity for sexual restraint.

You can't ever have everything that you want. This statement sounds simple and obvious, yet applying it in everyday living is quite difficult. At heart, we never completely outgrow our childish desires for omnipotence. Curiously, we want *all* the sex that we can get, *all* the attention that comes our way, and *all* the pleasure possible, without restriction. Only slowly and painfully do we recognize that complete fulfillment of our desires is impossible, and that every situation requires making a choice, selecting one thing and giving up another. It is impossible to be in two places at the same time even though both would seem equally attractive to you. If it were possible for you to travel quickly back and forth between them, you would never get to know and enjoy either. This is also true in attempting to maintain various relationships. As a promiscuous man or woman you may want sex whenever it is offered to you. Perhaps you feel you can achieve a certain amount of fulfillment this way. I don't believe you truly can, for in my therapeutic practice I have seen too many patients who have been rendered miserable by this way of life. For a while it may be possible to be on intimate terms with two or more individuals. However, in the long run you may find that whatever happiness you establish in one relationship deducts from the other.

Let me briefly outline the plot of a movie which demonstrates what I am trying to convey to you. A sea-captain led a double life. He was married to a woman who satisfied his needs for domesticity, comfort, and stability. His sea trips, however, regularly led him to a city where he kept company with a girl who fulfilled the needs left unsatisfied by his marriage—his desire for adventure and excitement. At the end of the movie the captain was "lost." His wife wanted to divorce him, and the adventurous girl in the foreign port pressed him for marriage. Caught in this dilemma, he was unable to hold on to either woman and lost the affection and love of both.

It is not for me to convert you to a different way of living. If you want to change, however, and don't know how to do so you may give some consideration to the thoughts that are suggested here. When new temptations arise, I would advise you *not* to make an appeal to your moral sense or will power. Instead, try to feel and anticipate right then and there, as vividly as you can, the most agonizing consequences imaginable. Again, in such situations, do not appeal to your conscience or your guilt, but to your own sense of self-preservation.

Perhaps you are a *real* Casanova and not deterred by these considerations. After all, he found much pleasure in life and became famous into the bargain. And after he had lost much of his attraction for women, writing his memoirs made it easier for him to bear his old age. But can you be sure that you will have Casanova's powers of observation and reflection and his ability to write when *your* old age approaches?

Will what I have said here help you to curb your sexual desires if you have been living promiscuously for a long time? If you are married and find yourself repeatedly involved in extramarital affairs, can you suddenly stop philandering? If you have tried to be faithful to one woman or one man but are unable to practice what you preached to yourself, will you try to change as the result of what you have read here? Will you be strong when the next temptation arises, perhaps more seductively than even before? I am not certain whether you will or not. We know what we should do and what is reasonable to do; however, when an unusual opportunity comes up we often fall right back on old habits, regardless of good resolutions.

If you doubt your ability to stick to your good intentions, my suggestion would be to read over what has been said so far—and then to read it over once again.

CHAPTER 17

Unhappy
Love

Lovesickness is the only illness which people do not get tired of, which they wish for as long as they live, and for which there will probably never be a completely effective cure. This, of course, does not imply that you must be sick to be in love (though the large number of people who nowadays consult psychotherapists because something has gone wrong with their love-lives makes one suspect that). However, there seems to be no question that some individuals love in a more healthy and less neurotic way than others. This chapter is meant to help you avoid some of the more neurotic pitfalls of love while you still can (perhaps during the early stages of love). I said "*more* neurotic pitfalls," for I believe that people who are in love *are* neurotic to some extent.

Of course, it is very difficult, if not outright futile, to give advice to a person who has succumbed to love fever. Such a role is like that of a minister preaching to a deaf congregation. Nevertheless, here are a few suggestions delivered in the spirit of preventive medicine.

Don't make your whole life dependent upon the person you love. What could be more natural than to want to do this! Love seems to be the only situation in which people can be genuinely altruistic. Even experiments with monkeys and other primates have shown that the males will restrain their appetites during the period of heat, and give whatever peanuts are available to the females (unfortunately this unselfish state is sharply curtailed after the courtship period is over).

The desire to make oneself virtually a captive or prisoner of the person with whom one is in love is particularly strong in inferiority-ridden people with somewhat masochistic tendencies. Masochists are people who derive more satisfaction from suffering than from enjoyment. Though psychotherapists used to think that masochistic tendencies were more characteristic of the female than the male, recent professional experience seems to suggest that there is no shortage of male masochists. If you are of this self-sacrificing type of individual, you must learn to check this basically unhealthy drive in yourself right at the beginning of a love relationship.

Therefore, I would advise you very strongly *not* to give up or neglect all your previous friendships and acquaintances, *not* to change your schedule of work and leisure activities to suit that of your lover. In other words, retain (for the sake of the person you love) some of your individual characteristics and follow some of your usual pursuits. Be *someone* to love, not merely a reflection. The ability to hold your own when you are confronted with another relationship is called *ego-strength* by therapists. To possess it, even to a moderate degree, is considered a sign of good mental stamina and health.

It is possible that your need to surrender yourself unconditionally to the person whom you love and to gain approval through blind compliance and self-sacrifice was a strategy that you had to develop as a child, in order to assure yourself of the continued love of your parents. To act this way may have been appropriate then, but as an adult there is no need to continue this pattern. Since the person whom you love is not your parent, to seek affection through self-sacrifice and obedience is no longer necessary. Moreover, such an attitude could also create feelings of humiliation and unconscious hostility which may arise whenever your self-effacing attitude is not rewarded by love and attention.

Making someone you love the center of your universe and letting all your activities orbit around your idol will be welcomed at first. However, after a while, your lover may resent such an attitude as a curtailment of freedom. Leading someone else's life instead of your own robs you of some of those original characteristics that made you appealing and interesting to your lover in the beginning.

Realize that premature and hasty sex fulfillment can sometimes destroy love. In former times, when social and religious standards were more rigidly fixed and adhered to, the problem of sexual fulfillment in love did not loom so large. Even today, in our freer culture, many people are torn between moral codes which they have been taught by others and those which grow out of their own thinking and feeling. Yet the pull toward the sexual relationship between people in love is strong and often irresistible, regardless of some of society's taboos.

If you are very much in love, and the urge to follow your sexual desires is strong, immediate initiation of a sexual relationship can establish a closeness and intimacy that strengthens the relationship. However, many love relationships that can develop into something quite meaningful and lasting are thrown out of gear by a hasty and premature sexual move. The premature physical consummation of a love affair can have the irreparable result of leading you to fall into sex, but out of love.

It is often not sufficiently realized that there can be serene beauty and unique charm to love before it has been ruffled by the fires of sexual involvement. Not that such a relationship could continue this way indefinitely, or that it should, but such a period of "banked fires" can serve a purpose. There can be no better preparation for future sexual satisfaction than a period of time which gives couples in love an opportunity to build a firm foundation of shared feelings and thoughts, before the element of sex is introduced into the relationship. Should something go wrong with their physical compatibility, the ensuing disappointment and frustration would be less painful.

So, if you are at all concerned with the future, do not rush too quickly from a friendly and tender love relationship into one that is primarily sexual. Also, do not think that you are less a male or female because at first you adopt a cautious attitude. Psychologists believe that an overeager and too impatient need for sex often masks a compensatory desire to prove one's own sexual prowess. Thus it is not necessarily a sign of virility or strong sexual responsiveness.

Don't make a slave of the person you love. Though slavery in the U.S. was abolished one hundred years ago, some of its features still seem to be prevalent in the love relationship.

The desire to possess the man or woman you love is a very natural tendency and, within limits, this desire is perfectly normal and justifiable. However, the neurotic lover who has been robbed of love countless times (or *thinks* he has) feels compelled to guard and bind his sweetheart. To his neurotic way of thinking, dominating the person he loves and denying him or her other influences, gives the relationship a measure of emotional security. However, a dictator is never lovable. The frequent and successful rebellions of many enslaved wives and husbands (often seeking a divorce for this very reason) seem to contradict the power of enslavement as a theory of love.

Therefore, if you detect in yourself even moderate characteristics of a love tyrant, attempt to curb such traits before the person whom you are trying to enslave becomes aware of them too, and stops loving you. Many men and women *want* to be enslaved and strongly dominated at the *beginning* of a relationship. But when they become fully aware of all of the restrictions of their situation, they do rebel.

Control, direction, and leadership will enhance feelings of admiration and affection. But use too much dominance, and love will evaporate as though it had never existed. Individuals who feel secure do not have to prove their power by chaining others down.

Don't let hostility in love upset you. Expect it and accept it. If you have fallen in love and seriously so, you may just as well reconcile yourself to the fact that along with its pleasures you will have to face a certain amount of hostility within yourself and in the person whom you love. Only in fairytales and in some of the older Hollywood movies does love exist in a pure and un-adulterated form without its share of hate and resentment.

I believe that hate and hostility in love are mainly defensive measures. When emotions run high, and the possibility of frustration and deprivation become a threat, the only way in which the individual affected can keep up his pride and self-esteem is by "falling into hate" with the loved person, thus saving his own pride and simultaneously discharging emotion. Happily, however, such hate and hostility is usually temporary, and is really in reaction to a specific situation, not in response to the person as a whole. Furthermore, lovers' quarrels and fights often serve to test and cement a still shaky relationship. Only if such fights continue indefinitely and become insoluble need they concern you more seriously.

It is important *not* to think that your newly established bond is hopelessly severed with the appearance of hostility. Hostility is an inevitable part of all living. If it has been completely absent so far, your love relationship is not a realistic one.

Don't fall prey to false idealization of your lover. Why we fall in love with a certain individual (usually not the one we are logically expected to love) still remains a mystery. However, most psychologists seem to agree that the whole process has something to do with the establishment of an ideal person in fantasy (referred to as ego-ideal). For a woman, "Mr. Ideal" may be a Marlon Brando type, a husky football hero, a sensitive artist, a gangster, or a noble prince of foreign descent. For a man, "Miss Ideal" may be projected in the form of a beauty-contest queen, an all-forgiving, all-understanding motherly woman, a sweet and homey type, or an exotically glamorous girl. The ideal person usually has some of those characteristics which you lack yourself.

What happens when you fall in love is this: you become aroused and delighted at meeting someone who comes close to the idealized image you have been worshiping all your life. Symbolically speaking, you begin to hang all kinds of decorations on this person, as if you were trimming a Christmas tree with stars and lights which you have saved from childhood.

This process of idealization can become quite dangerous unless it is checked early because it may lead you so far astray that you don't know whether you are in love with a figment of your imagination or with a live person.

Be aware of the fact that the men or women who we choose as lovers *have not asked to be our heroes and idealized images.* We should therefore not hold them responsible if they fall short of our expectations. One way to protect yourself against future disillusionment is to try to forget the idealized image, and to concentrate on learning to *know* your lover. You may find yourself delightfully surprised to discover that he or she is actually *more* wonderful than you had fantasized.

Don't let excess anxiety poison your love prematurely. Anxiety is primarily a human characteristic because it is tied up with the fact that as human beings we are aware that everything we do can come to an end, and that possibly bleak future events can terminate present pleasures.

People often react toward love with particularly strong feelings of anxiety, because love can change so quickly, and its substance seems so intangible. This is why we want continuous reassurance that we are truly loved, and why behind even the most secure love lurks the fear of its loss.

Yet nobody likes an overly anxious and continually questioning lover. It is possible to drive yourself nearly mad if you constantly worry about losing the love that you have found. Your concern may take the form of extreme and unreasonable jealousy, an insatiable need for reassurance, and a ceaseless desire for overt proof and clear demonstration that you and you alone are the one who is loved.

If you feel that you are caught in a vicious anxiety circle of this kind, you must try to realize that it is probably not your lover who is causing you such anxiety, but that you never felt very secure in the love of your parents, or that certain events occurred that made you fear your parents would abandon you. What you are doing now is re-enacting the old fear. No amount of reassurance from the person with whom you are now in love can help you as much as your own realization that you are over-reacting to a past and not to a present situation.

Try to substitute some kind of faith and trust for your anxiety. In love, *you* must offer security, faith, and trust in order to receive it from the other person. Even if the faith in the person whom you love is not fully justified sometimes, the fact that you extend it without always having a substantial basis for it will strengthen the other person's love for you. The individual who wants to invest trust and love only when he can be completely sure of the returns will find safe but often meager returns for his investment. The fact that others have faith in us, *even if our actions do not always justify it at first,* makes us feel more trustworthy ourselves, and more eager to remain so. Many fickle husbands and wives have been so disarmed by their partners' faith in them that they have been able to change some of their unstable characteristics. *Don't analyze love but enjoy it.* The anatomical dissection and analysis of love is not necessary unless something is radically wrong.

The fact that you are in love is a most wonderful thing. You are the envy of a large number of people who continually search for love and seem to have difficulty in finding it. It is, of course, very difficult to enjoy the feeling of love without wondering whether it will continue, what it will lead to if it does continue, and how it compares with the experiences of others. As in other areas of life, our human capacity to reason and to look into the future can be a curse as well as a blessing.

I believe that it is important to love with open eyes and with concern about the future. However, during the very early stages of a relationship it is equally essential to be able to enjoy love for what it is, not only what it will be, or could be. With all the heartaches, complications, fluctuations, uncertainties, and doubts that can be involved, you must be determined to enjoy the experience of love. Your will to enjoy it instead of destroying it by excess *neurotic* tendencies will keep you from becoming too lovesick, just as the physically sick patient's attitude toward his disease often makes the difference between being healthy or ill.

CHAPTER **18**   Rejection

Someone you love has rejected you; someone whom you thought loved you. A relationship which gave meaning and warmth to your life has suddenly ceased. Possibly your first impulse is to find someone else, a new lover who *really* appreciates you, but this can spell danger. Entering into a new love relationship too quickly after you have been hurt may be more damaging than helpful. You may discover that the new love does not measure up to the old, and your disappointment and frustration at this may only plunge you further into despair and depression. A patient of mine once had a bad experience in this regard. Unexpectedly jilted by her fiancé, she attempted to soothe the pain of this emotional blow, by quickly accepting an invitation to dinner. She spent a most miserable evening! The young man misunderstood her need for affection and tried to seduce her, making her feel even worse than before.

Perhaps your friends advise you to get away from it all. Take a vacation; a cruise if you have the money; a moderately priced resort if you are on a tight budget. Think this over carefully. You may pack your suitcase to escape, but the last thing you'll unpack when you get there is yourself. The person with a broken heart who takes an ocean trip or seeks the solace of the countryside to escape from problems, often finds that what he was trying to forget only returns with greater force. Someone who has been hurt emotionally is not likely to enter quickly into the gay spirit of cruise life. Nor is he too eager to be drawn into the games and diversions planned by the social director of a summer resort. So before you take hasty and foolish steps to get over your disappointment and rejection, pause a moment and try to examine the causes that could have led to the broken relationship.

Did you, unwittingly, want to be rejected? Don't dismiss this possibility to quickly. People often *think* they want to be loved and yet reject love at the same time. This may sound contradictory, but stop to consider that any close relationship, as well as giving joy, demands some sacrifice. It means giving up a certain amount of freedom, living up to expectations and responsibilities, and even facing the possibility of being hurt.

> I am reminded of Fred, a patient of mine who became distraught when his girl friend suddenly broke off with him. He claimed that he loved her more than anything else in the world, yet when they were together, he had continually argued with her over trifles: whether it was quicker to take the bus or the car, the correct spelling of words, whether a color was pink or just pale red. When he gave her presents they were usually the wrong things: an oversized pocketbook, a novel she had already read, a scarf that was the wrong color. You don't have to be a psychologist to see that he was trying to get rid of her all the time. And then, when she did finally leave him, he thought it was she who was doing the rejecting.

Have you been too critical? Perhaps you acted like a cranky schoolteacher with your lover, constantly demanding perfection and correcting faults, instead of attempting to understand them. Nobody likes to be criticized. One is exposed to enough criticism at work and from one's family members. It is

167

important to realize that there are few perfect things in life. Even the finest gold bracelet is not pure gold, and the strongest alcohol is not one hundred per cent alcohol when you drink it. You may have been rejected in your relationship because you were too much of a perfectionist.

Have you been too sensitive? It may be that because you were bossed by your mother or father when you were young, you cannot stand such behavior in others, and are quick to believe that they are trying to control you. Would you allow a past childhood situation to interfere with present relationships? Of course not, but you may have been doing just that. There is an infantile streak left in us all that usually comes up at the most inopportune time.

Have you been too demanding and impatient? One can often be impatient when it comes to important things, and yet display an angel's endurance with regard to unessential matters. Perhaps you tried to *rush* the relationship, and it was this that led to your rejection. If you think so, try to recall some of the great romantic novels and stories in world literature and legend. Remember how the love story develops gradually, and how this adds to the suspense and excitement. It may be essential for you to realize that important relationships need time to grow and to develop, much like trees or plants whose growth you can't push.

Is your rejection really final? Is it possible that you have called it quits to soon? Though you may think the final curtain has descended on your "love drama," the break in your relationship may actually only represent the intermission. Possibly the person who rejected and left you merely acted in a sudden fit of temper. Perhaps he or she is sitting at home right now, waiting for you to call and make up. Leaving you may also have been a way of testing the strength of your relationship. Could it be that only you and not your lover has accepted this test as a final one?

Now, after you have mulled over all these considerations carefully, you must decide whether you want to mend your

168

broken tie. Don't continue with the relationship unless you feel really sure you want to, and have some understanding of what went wrong. If you are certain that you can patch things up and proceed with a little more understanding, don't waste time in playing the part of the rejected lover. Swallow your pride, and make a fresh start in something that was never really over to begin with.

If, on the other hand, you feel that there is no chance to recapture what you have lost or to repair the damage, here are some thoughts that may help you to bear the brunt of your disappointment and frustration.

Realize that you are not alone in experiencing grief and anger in a situation of this kind. Life is a continuous process of being sometimes at the giving end and sometimes at the receiving. There is no individual, no matter how wise and successful, who has not at some time, been rejected in love. Every rejection has within it a lesson that can help make for wiser behavior in the future.

Since your feelings have been hurt, try to court other positive emotional experiences. Only you can tell what they might be. Buy the best seats for a baseball game or the theater. Get a goldfish, a cat or a dog, or a new set of curtains. Buy a new dress or a set of golf clubs. Does painting, sculpture, or photography appeal to you? Or perhaps you'd rather take a course in literature, psychology, or history. Whatever activity you think you might find especially rewarding is worth trying—particularly if it also provides a creative outlet. Perhaps you have heard the story of how Goethe, the famous German author, reacted when he was frustrated in love. He was so unhappy about his experience that he contemplated suicide. Instead, he decided to write a novel in which he had the *hero* kill himself because he was deprived of the woman he loved. But Goethe himself remained very much alive. By pouring his frustration into the written word, he cured himself of his own feelings of rejection. True, you are not Goethe and may not have his talents, but nothing prevents you from profiting from his experience.

Recognize that at least ninety per cent of your present grief, frustration, and anger is due to hurt pride. It is very important for you to understand that your bad luck in this one relationship does not mean that you are worthless as a person, or not worthy of being loved. With this thought in my mind, boost your ego! Be nice to yourself, nicer than you usually are. For a while, be just a little more patient with yourself, with your mistakes and shortcomings, than usual. Treat yourself as you would a convalescent patient, with kindness and firmness, but not with self-pity. Since you have been rejected in love, you must try twice as hard now not to make matters worse by also rejecting yourself.

Don't be impatient if your cure takes time and effort. Your own attitude can do much to shorten the period of recovery.

PART FOUR

Parent-Child

Crises

CHAPTER 19

Crisis
After Childbirth

You feel depressed instead of overjoyed. Probably, you looked forward to, in fact counted the months and finally days till your child's arrival. Though you were doubtless somewhat afraid of the act of childbirth, it never occurred to you that you could be upset and depressed *after* your child's birth.

It *is* possible for you as a mother to be depressed and unhappy after the birth of your baby, in spite of the fact that you may have wanted this child with all your heart and soul. If you feel this way, it may help you to know that such a reaction is not abnormal when you consider what may have led up to it. Here are some of the causes of the "baby blues." Knowing and understanding them may take some of the edge off your despondency.

First, giving birth is a situation of stress and danger, physically as well as emotionally. Some individuals react to such situations with depression by internalizing the pressure and tension involved. You too may be prone to the depression syndrome, but it will pass as soon as the aftereffects of the delivery begin to wear off. The depression syndrome is determined by partly physiological and partly psychological conditions. Under these conditions you feel sad, dejected, inactive, and "low" without apparent reason.

Second, you should realize that the birth of your child is an event that you have anticipated for many months with such eagerness that it has become exaggerated and distorted in your fantasy. Now, when the child has finally actually been born, the event doesn't seem as glamorous as you had pictured it during your pregnancy. As a result, you feel somewhat disappointed or mildly let down. We often feel that way when something that we have built up in imagination suddenly comes true. This is a very natural reaction and you should not allow to let it upset you. It is the process of adjusting to reality, at first somewhat painful and disappointing, yet becoming easier as time goes on.

Chemical changes affect your body for three months *after* the birth of your baby, as the body readjusts to its postpregnancy state, in much the same way as the body reacted to changing needs in your *first* three months of pregnancy. These changes may affect your mood. Just try to slide with the moods, not taking them seriously, and remembering that they may be the result of the bodily adjustments. You are tired from labor as well as emotionally let down after all the attention and fuss of the hospital.

You may also find yourself prey to feelings of helplessness in the face of all the tasks which you must undertake. Try to organize your time, *and always make sure that you have one hour a day of complete rest and solitude, for the first two weeks.* After this period of adjustment you'll most probably find things settling into a pleasant routine, and you'll wonder what life was like before the baby. Should you not start feeling better after six weeks, speak to your obstetrician about yourself. He'll be sure to have some helpful suggestions.

It is also very important to get away now and then to regain your perspective and to have some time alone with your husband.

You don't really love your newborn child. What a horrible and upsetting thought. It goes against everything that you have been taught about mother-child relationships. You may not dare to admit to yourself that your child is *not* the sweetest, the most

174

lovable, the most beautiful and attractive infant in this world. However, deep down in your unconscious mind there may be a lack of expected maternal warmth toward this little bundle of flesh and diapers that is part of yourself and yet seems so different. This lack of "real" mother love may even continue for the following days of nursing.

If such emotions of detachment and even of slight hostility take hold of you and cast a shadow over what are supposed to be some of your most happy days and hours, try not to repress or deny them but realize that these feelings do not exclude the simultaneous presence of love and affection. Be aware of the fact that there are other mothers who feel somewhat ill at ease about their infants *at first,* although such "evil" thoughts and ideas will rarely be expressed or admitted. Since so much of a baby's first weeks of life are spent sleeping, and demands for attention are largely physiological, it may be quite difficult to be carried off your feet emotionally by the little girl or boy who either annoys you or pays no attention to you whatsoever.

In essence, then, don't be alarmed or disappointed if your strong and very genuine affection for your child is not *immediately* present.

You doubt whether you really have what it takes to be a good mother. Although you have read all the child-parent manuals and perhaps have taken courses in child psychology, you feel helpless and incompetent with your child. For example, when your baby gets the hiccups, you are frantic and think he may suffocate. Eventually, you begin to fear that you are about as qualified for motherhood as a monkey is to play a violin. If worry about this affects your peace of mind, derive consolation and support from the following *facts:*

(a) *Every* first-time mother is a novice at her task of infant care and, as such, she cannot be expected to do a *perfect* job.

(b) There are many aspects of infant care that you can only learn through your own experience.

175

(c) Your anxiety and insecurity are probably the remnants of an old inferiority complex that goes back to your childhood. Forget the past and face the present with faith and confidence in your own judgment. After all, this is *your child,* and who can know better than you how to treat him.

You feel slightly irritated at your family. Having been the number-one person in your life, your husband could easily feel now that he is playing a secondary if not subordinate role. Try to understand when he gets slightly angry at having to wait for his breakfast longer than usual, or if the satisfaction of your baby's needs take precedence over his. Although it is up to him, too, to understand and to accept the situation and to make the adjustment, you can aid him greatly by giving him extra attention and love during the trying first months after your child has been born.

There may also be a strong desire on the part of the older and supposedly more experienced members of your family (mother, aunt, grandmother, and mother-in-law) to take over and to overwhelm you with advice and suggestions as to the best way of handling your infant. Although you are undoubtedly grateful for their care, you probably can't help being slightly annoyed at times when your relatives act as if the child belongs to them exclusively. Be tactful but firm. You should not let them take the reins out of your hands, or allow them to confuse you about what is right or wrong for your baby. The old saying that "mother knows best" is probably appropriate here, though it refers to you, not to your mother. Naturally, profit from the practical experience of other mothers and be kind and grateful for their desire to make life a little easier for you now. But realize that no two children or two mothers are ever exactly alike. In many situations that involve your child, your own intuition and your common sense judgment will be your best guide.

You are worried about your baby's future development. Nobody can tell you with absolute certainty at this point whether your child will grow up to become a genius, a prophet, a stock broker, a future Madame Curie, a failure in business or school, an artist or a happy housewife, a strong or weak person.

Although there are some psychological tests that claim to gauge an infant's future intelligence almost hours after birth, most of these measures are unreliable. Every baby develops, to some extent, according to his own individual pattern, and the rate of development is often not predictable. Your pediatrician should be consulted if you think there is something basically wrong with your infant's mentality and behavior. But if the doctor gives you a clean bill of health for the child, you need not worry. Even if there are some deficiencies or symptoms, just what course they will take in the future (for better or worse) is usually an enigma, even to the greatest experts in child care and development.

Naturally, you want to do everything possible to further your child's healthy development and to make sure that you live up to your own image of a good mother. But your desire to be *perfect* can lead you to become overly anxious and overly concerned. Furthermore, if you feel that you have to respond to your child's every need at the sacrifice of your own needs and comfort, the resulting inner tension and resentment may be highly detrimental. You should realize that even during the early stages of development, your child has to learn that *his desires can and should not always be satisfied instantly and completely.* You will best prepare him for the future if he can learn this lesson while he is still young, even though he may at times feel frustrated. He may be *more* frustrated if this lesson has to be learned at a later stage of his development.

The art of bringing up a child is to find a happy medium between the satisfaction of your own needs as an individual and the fulfillment of your obligations as a mother.

CHAPTER **20** / The
Runaway Child

"Johnny—get in touch with us immediately. All is forgiven and forgotten. We love you and want to see you back home. Mom and Dad."

"Call us any time. Your father does not mind if you use the car. Do come back, Billy. We are lost without you. Your loving parents."

Notices of this kind in the newspapers often make one wonder what lies behind them. The emotional tone of such advertisements is probaby merely a faint reflection of a previous family drama. One can almost picture the parents anxiously awaiting the return of the errant son or daughter. Why do children run away from home? What makes them do it?

THE PSYCHOLOGICAL BACKGROUND

It is not uncommon to react to major crises and emergencies by running away from them. However, in the case of a child who decamps from home the flight from danger is a literal one, highlighting the urgency of the situation. Obviously, if a young person decides to pack up and leave home he must have compelling reasons for taking such an extreme step. In my experience as a psychotherapist, the following are some of the causes which I have found lead children and adolescents to run away from home:

The deserter wants to punish his parents for lack of atten-

tion and love. This is particularly true in the case of young people who have been treated with indifference at home. By running away they want to create a dramatic situation that puts
them into the limelight. A patient of mine who had run away
from home told me that she did it mainly to find out whether her
career-woman mother would even *notice* that her daughter had
gone away for a day or two. Secretly the young girl hoped that
her departure would teach the mother to be more attentive.

Others who forsake the safety of a home abruptly resort to
this measure to prove their independence. What they want to
convey to their parents indirectly is: "See—I can get along without you! I am far more independent and capable than you think.
I can take care of myself." A youngster who has been overly dominated at home is most apt to leave on the basis of such thinking.

In still other instances young people run away in order to
force their parents to allow a privilege that has been denied to
them. This may involve anything from dating or marrying someone who has been *person non grata* to using the family car. Adolescents who are stubborn and have been spoiled in childhood
are often prone to run away in the hope that this dramatic act
will sway their parents to grant their wishes.

Regardless of the underlying causes, when a child runs
away from home it is almost always a serious psychological indication that there is something basically wrong with the parent-
child relationship. Therefore, if your child has left you, you must
re-examine your parental attitudes very carefully.

If there are indications that a lack of *attention* or love has
caused your child to desert you, it may be that you were dem-
onstrative only at your own whim or convenience, and not when
your child was most in need of affection. Perhaps you only *half*-
listened to him when he talked about his problems. Or maybe
the child's brother or sister received the major portion of your
love and interest.

Should your son's or daughter's sudden departure from

home have been triggered by an excessive need to prove youthful *independence,* chances are that you have been overprotective or you may have neglected to gradually loosen the reins of parental control while your child was growing older and entitled to increasing independence. Your need to overprotect your child may be a projection of *your own* anxiety about life and the future and not truly anxiety about your child.

Try to be freer and more relaxed in this respect in the future. Of course you can't give *unlimited* freedom to a youngster, but nevertheless make concessions to his need to be independent whenever you reasonably can.

If your child has run away in order to *force you* to give up one of your demands or to alter a decision, your situation is comparable to that of a ruler of a country who is confronted with a revolution against a regime that is conceived of as unfair. Perhaps you ruled too sternly. Of course, there are instances in which you as a parent are not to blame at all, and other factors not directly connected with your home environment are the major cause of your child's sudden flight from home. This could be particularly true if children are strongly under the influence of friends or companions, or if they have formed a passionate attachment to a person or environment from which they have been removed against their will. The parent may not be the primary source of the trouble if the child who is running away from home is known to suffer from an emotional disturbance which manifests itself by poor reality contact or by attention, concentration, or intelligence disturbances. If such is the case, the act of disappearance is not psychologically significant in itself but only a link in a chain of symptoms. Incidentally, it should be mentioned here that the kind of emotional disturbance which is known as "fugue" and which is characterized by a person's sudden leaving of familiar surroundings and going on a trip to a strange locality in a kind of daze, is more frequently encountered among adults than among children and adolescents.

Naturally, to restore harmony to a poor parent-child relationship takes time and patience. However, here are some suggestions for the immediate emergency situation.

Forget all the stories that you have read about rape, murder, seduction, and crime in connection with young people! True, the world is always full of evil and perhaps the young and the inexperienced are more easily prey to it than the mature adult. However, dangerous people and influences are present all the time. Just because your child is away from the protection of your home does not mean that he or she is helpless or lost. When an emergency occurs, imagination often works overtime. Perhaps as a protection against what *might* happen, one is inclined to imagine the worst. Thus you may picture your child walking the dark alleys of the city while actually he is treating himself to his favorite ice-cream, and wondering when to go home.

Try to remember that there is a mature and reasonable streak in the most irresponsible young adult and that this rational aspect of the personality (psychologists call it the *superego*) will tend to keep your child from getting into serious trouble. Also, has it occurred to you that your child may miss the comfort and protection of home and may therefore become more appreciative of them? Try to direct your thoughts along these and similar lines, and it will put a damper on your worries and keep your imagination from jumping to dire conclusions.

Many parents feel that they must notify the police as soon as they have discovered that their "darling" has left domestic bed and board. *Don't do this at once!* Such action is often a premature and false step and one which may be regretted later. (Of course, make an exception in the case of the emotionally handicapped child.) Chances are that such a move will make the runaway feel like a delinquent. Apprehension and return by police officers will only serve to enhance his feelings of hostility against you as a parent. He will resent you for taking so drastic a measure as informing the police, and will also interpret it as a sign of your own helplessness or just another punitive measure.

Should your child communicate with you by phone during your anxious waiting period, act as calm and composed as you can under the circumstances. Without giving him the third degree in the way of questions, make him feel that he will be welcome home any time.

When the prodigal daughter or son finally returns, accept him or her at first without making too much of a fuss over what has happened and why it has occurred. Eventually, however, every effort should be made to get at the basic psychological factors that were responsible for this act.

A fundamental change in your attitude and in your relationship with your child may be required to prevent a recurrence of the unfortunate incident. If you can't accomplish this by yourself, don't hesitate to seek professional assistance. A comforting final thought: follow-up statistics have demonstrated that runaways rarely repeat the experience a second time, if an honest attempt is made to correct the cause for flight.

CHAPTER 21

The Child
Who Fails in School

"Johnny is improving in his school work, but he is still not working up to his capacity. He could do better but he is not trying hard enough."

"On the basis of your letter, we have given most careful attention to your situation. However, we regret to inform you that Patricia has again failed all her subjects this term. Therefore we shall be unable to readmit her to school for the fall semester."

Naturally, parents are desperate when they receive news of this kind. "Nowadays you need an education even to get a job as a garbage collector," I was told by a mother whose son had just failed all his courses. "What is he going to do later on in life without a high-school diploma?" Many parents feel about education as this mother did, and develop a severe case of "exam jitters" when their children's grades drop lower and lower. What can parents do in such a situation? Where can they turn for help?

Since I have had the opportunity to counsel parents who have been in this unfortunate dilemma, let me now try to convey to you some of the suggestions that I have given to them. When I am confronted with parents of failing students, I usually try first to point out some basic facts about the psychology of learning and studying. Here they are in a condensed form:

Studying takes more than intelligence or I.Q. Why? First, because studying is an activity that usually requires solitude and isolation, and few people like to be alone for a prolonged period of time. Young people especially dislike it. Second, the successful student must possess an exceptional amount of self-discipline. But all discipline is difficult; self-discipline even more so. It is a capacity that is slowly developed over the years. Third, the rewards earned for academic studies are usually in the future, not in the present. For example, it is hard for many young people to see why they should have to memorize irregular French verbs when they may never visit France and have a chance to speak the language. It takes much maturity to work for long-range goals.

All learning requires special self-confidence. To master any skill takes a certain amount of almost blind courage and confidence to counteract the possibility of failure which is inherent in every learning situation. If confidence has already been damaged during the early years of childhood, it is difficult to develop it later on in school. In fact, an *exceptional* amount of confidence is required for school work because many of the elementary skills which are taught in education are entirely new for the student. Since your child is confronted by them *for the first time,* he does not have the sense of security that is derived from previous experience and success, and therefore he may give up prematurely or fail.

Many young people react to their teachers in the same manner that they respond to their parents. How strict, lenient, or inconsistent our parents have been in teaching us some of the "basic lessons of life" (eating, learning how to walk, talk, take care of physical needs) leaves a lasting imprint for the future. Your child could hate school or may not want to study and learn because the teacher does not treat him in the same way as he was treated by his parents in the past. If the parent has been very strict during the early development period, the teacher too could be conceived of as an overly threatening father- or mother-figure. The fear aroused by this can make it impossible to concentrate and to pay attention. Similarly, the child who has been overindulged in preschool days will demand an undue amount of attention and rebel when the teacher does not spoon-feed education to him. It is important for young people to outgrow such attitudes, but it often takes time and patience to do it.

All of us are not as capable as we should be, therefore don't expect perfection from your child. Are you the *best* parent? As a father have you reached the summit of success in your occupation? As a mother are you always the epitome of parental wisdom and emotional control? Isn't it true that you often know exactly what you should do, but just the same find it difficult to do it? Ask yourself some of these questions and you may find that you really have no right to demand from your child a degree of perfection and maturity that you can't even maintain yourself.

It is important to look at your child's failure in school from his point of view, not only from your own. You, as a parent, realize the importance of education, perhaps because you have been severely handicapped by a lack of it in your career. Economic pressures and the hard knocks of life may have given you an early awareness of the social and financial disadvantages of the lack of an education, and therefore you find it difficult to understand why your child does not see it exactly your way. You are looking at the picture from *your* point of view, and on the basis of *your* past experience. Now try to look at the situation from your child's point of view.

Since he is younger than yourself, he has a different kind of metabolism that makes him often more restless and fidgety than you are. As the result of this he finds it more difficult to sit still and be confined to a room or a study hall. Being physically active, tossing a ball into a ring or driving a car provides more of a thrill for him than bending over a desk and engaging in purely mental gymnastics. Also, being younger than you are, he is more eager to learn from his own experience and exploration than from what teachers and books try to tell him about life. Furthermore, he wants to know about the world as it is today, not as it was yesterday or thousands of years ago, and much of what is taught in school is based on past experience.

Since your child has been exposed to a childhood environment that is different from yours, you can not compare his abilities and attitudes to those that you held when you were young.

Educational achievement is not everything: some children fail in school, yet succeed in life later on. Academic ability and future vocational skill do not always go together. It is true, of course, that there are some children who have a special knack for absorbing learning and as a result become great teachers, doctors, or lawyers. However, for every one of these academic prodigies, I could name you countless other people whose special talents remained untapped and unrecognized in school. Take a look at the educational backgrounds of some of our outstanding artists, writers, and successful businessmen. You will be amazed to find how many of them had difficult problems in school in their childhood. Though this may seem a rationalization, realize that not *"all* is lost when school is lost."

The parent is not always at fault. Many parents blame *themselves* too much when there is a succession of poor grades on the report cards of their children. This is due to the fact that teachers and—I am sorry to say—psychologists are often too quick to say to parents: "Mrs. Smith, *you* are pushing the child too much" or *"You* let him get away with too many things. It is all *your* fault."

Like many parents, you may have made serious *faux pas* in bringing up your children, and partly as the result of this they may have failed in school. This does not necessarily indicate that you are a *"bad"* parent, or that you are to blame *entirely.* Of course not. The disciplinary methods which you have used in "bringing up baby" may have been ill-advised, but they have probably been the best that you knew at the time and chances are that you have used them with the best of intentions. Remember that even eminent pediatricians and child psychologists make mistakes. Therefore, don't blame yourself excessively, and don't develop what is called a parental guilt complex. It will only make things more difficult if you do.

If your child should hate you at present because he senses how angry you are about his failure in school, don't allow this to unbalance you. Your failing son or daughter may actually feel resentful toward *himself* for what has happened, and then use you as a scapegoat to get over his own disappointment; for children too, are prone to *project* when things go wrong, and who could be better targets for projection than their own parents?

These are some of the basic psychological considerations which I think parents of failing students should keep in mind. What has been said are explanations of, not answers to, your problems. However, you must know *something* about the deeper causes and motives of troubles before you can cure them. Now the question arises, what *cures* are available in your present crisis? Let us examine closely some of the remedial measures that could be applied, and determine which one would be most appropriate for your specific situation. Here are some of the alternatives that are open to you.

CORRECTIVE METHODS

Leaving school. Should your child quit school, this way of handling the situation may leave you cold or furious as a parent, whereas your child might be overjoyed at the prospect. The thought of being relieved from the burden of schoolwork and examinations, and holding a paid job instead, can have tremendous appeal for many young people.

As a parent of a high-school child, consider this: If your child quits school now for a prolonged period of time, he may eventually lose interest in it altogether. His already weak motivation to educate himself may, once he gives up school altogether, fade out completely. However, for the failing college student, a leave of absence from school, and a job during the interim period may be the right step.

In many colleges, advisers have discovered that, after they have had a chance to be "on their own," some of their problem students have come back to their studies with a more mature attitude. The same does not always hold true for high-school students who have fewer opportunities for obtaining jobs, and who may not yet possess the emotional maturity to profit from employment experience.

Some parents think that having their children sign up for the Army or Navy is the solution, hoping that such experience will teach their youngsters those lessons of discipline that they were unable to absorb at home or in school. This expectation is fulfilled *sometimes*. However, in most other instances problem students also become problem sailors or soldiers. In a military environment young people learn how to take orders and how to accept discipline from an outside authority. Yet they may fail to develop the special kind of *self-discipline* that is important for work and study. In general, most experience seems to indicate that the military services do not always make men out of immature adolescents and young adults.

Letting a young person quit school to give him a chance to learn from outside experience may be feasible only after several other remedial measures have been tried.

Change to another school. This may be advisable if the school which your child attends at present is overcrowded or maintains excessively high or low academic standards. There are poor schools and poor teachers. I believe that most academic failure is not the teacher's fault, but is caused by the young student's *own attitudes* and *study habits*. It is often easy to blame it all on the educational system. However, if your heart is set on a change of school, here are some pointers on how to go about it:

(1) Be sure to *prepare* your child for the transfer and try

188

to get his co-operation for such a change of school. If he rebels too much, he will enter the new school with a chip on his shoulder and offer resistance to learning which could lower his grades again.

(2) Visit several of the new schools that have been recommended to you *with your child* and select the one that he likes best provided it also meets with your approval. He, not only you, must like the new school in order to succeed in it later on. In finding the right school, you may be aided greatly by consulting one of the educational agencies that specialize in placing children and adolescents in the right kind of educational environment. You'll find them listed in the classified telephone book.

(3) When you visit a boarding or preparatory school, don't be unduly impressed by the external trimmings. Magnificent buildings and grounds, lovely classrooms, and the most modern educational equipment are certainly nice, but more important than these exteriors are personalities and qualifications of the teaching personnel, the size of the school classes (teacher-student ratio), the amount of individual attention given to students, and the over-all educational philosophy and approach of the school. You can try to investigate through parents whose children are currently enrolled in the place where you plan to register your child.

(4) Don't think that because a school is "parochial" or "military" this *necessarily* means that instruction will be better or academic standards will be higher. This may be so sometimes, but much depends upon the particular school you select.

Try private tutoring. Private tutoring can be helpful if your child has a poor background in one or several of the basic educational subjects. This may have been due to repeated class absences, or frequent changing of schools in the past. This remedial step is also advisable if your child is an intellectually handicapped student who takes more time and individual attention to absorb the materials covered in class.

If this is the case, make a special effort to choose the *right* tutor. Try to find a person for this job who is not only academically competent, but who also has a personality that appeals to your child. A bright college student (perhaps not too far removed in years from your child in age) may often be preferable to a Ph.D. who could be taking the job mainly to earn some extra income during his spare time. Should your child come to *like* his tutor, there is no limit to what he could learn. Then such experience could almost have a therapeutic value. If, on the other hand, he hates or feels indifferent toward his tutor, he will not improve, and the money you have spent on tutoring will be wasted.

If you yourself are in good command of the three R's, you may be tempted to tutor your child. This, in my opinion, can be a serious mistake, even though you may be principal of the local high school or personnel supervisor in a large industrial firm. You may be your child's *worst* tutor because of your emotional involvement with your child, and because of his involvement with you as a parent. You may be too impatient, set too high standards, and having been taught differently yourself, not realize what is expected of children in school today. This does not mean that you must refuse to help your child with his homework when he requests it. There is bound to be some emotional confusion if a student has to follow two masters—the "school master" and the "master at home." Incidentally, I advise *against* private tutoring if your child is very intelligent, and is in command of the necessary knowledge. If his problem is primarily due to laziness, a tutor may merely function in the role of a person who is supporting your child's need to have someone else do his work. He will come to lean on this crutch too often and lose his own initiative.

Does your child need remedial reading? If it can be demonstrated on the basis of tests that your child has a deficient vocabulary, that his rate of comprehension is too slow, and that he can't grasp what he reads, remedial reading instruction could be one of the solutions to your child's school problems.

Nowadays, there is a tendency to overemphasize the importance of remedial reading, and to look at it as an all-out cure for learning and study problems, which it is not. Bringing up your child's reading speed and comprehension should only be looked at as a preliminary step. Your child may become the world's fastest reader, and master all the required reading comprehension techniques, but yet continue to prefer the funnies to an encyclopedia or read only the sports page of the newspaper.

How to arouse your child's interest in better and more refined kind of reading? A difficult task. Try to avoid one mistake: Don't tell him he should be more interested in reading merely *because you as a parent happen to like it.* A love for books, like all forms of love, cannot be forced. Basically, it stems from emotional rather than intellectual needs. It is important, therefore, to appeal to your child's feelings and desires if you want to make a bookworm out of him, or at least stir his interest in books. Along this vein, try to communicate to him somehow that books are living replicas of what people have experienced. Convey that the knowledge derived from reading can also serve to make him a more interesting conversationalist and person. Demonstrate to him that reading can enable him to get more fun out of life. In short, attempt to appeal to his own pleasure principle to arouse interest in books. I realize that to accomplish this may be as difficult as converting an agnostic to a Christian Scientist. This is hard, but it is nevertheless not impossible.

Psychotherapy may be the needed aid. While most parents may not object to sending their children to a remedial reading course or to having them privately tutored, many a child's father or mother will often be severely shocked if psychotherapy is suggested for a youngster who fails in school.

This reaction is very understandable, for despite the popular realization of psychology and psychiatry, there is still an ancient stigma attached to psychotherapy, because in many people's minds it is associated with extreme cases of insanity, or with commitment to a mental institution. On the other hand, there are also those parents who are *oversold* on what psychology accomplishes. They think that just having their children "analyzed" will make them mature at once and enable them eventually to earn that place on the school's honor roll which they really deserve on the basis of their capabilities.

Both attitudes toward therapy are, of course, extreme and misleading. As so often, somewhere in the middle of these extremes is the right approach. Giving your child an opportunity to discuss some of his personal and school problems with an objective and yet warm and understanding individual (that is what a good psychotherapist really is) could have many beneficial effects. On the other hand, one must realize that psychotherapy, like any kind of treatment, does not *always* work with every child or adolescent. There is an element of chance that you must be willing to take, if your child sees a therapist. Realize that the beneficial and tangible effects of therapeutic treatment often take time to materialize and you can't always expect *quick* and immediate changes. Don't go by what *other* parents have told you about therapy and *their* children, for every child and adolescent is different, and responds differently to various situations.

Your whole concept of psychotherapy may be based on false premises. It may be important for you to realize that there are different kinds of therapeutic treatment. Psychological treatment does not always take many years, is not all based on sex, and nowadays the couch is rarely used for patients. The treatment is not so expensive that you have to take a loan or deplete your bank account to be able to afford it. There are many young people who can be helped considerably through counseling (which is a form of therapy) by a competent psychologist or psychiatrist. It is, of course, true that many confused young people outgrow their problems (particularly those problems that are connected with school and learning) through the natural process of maturation. However, maturing can sometimes be speeded up and be made less painful with the aid of psychotherapy.

A final consideration: You may be firmly convinced that therapy is good for your child, but *he may be dead-set against it.* This is natural for him. Most of us hate to admit our failures and problems, and even more, to have them exposed to us by others. This holds true for many adults, and especially so for young people, who in addition may think they are abnormal or queer if they have to see a psychiatrist or psychologist.

If this situation occurs, explain to your child that seeking psychological help does not mean that he is crazy, or in fact any different from other people. Tell him that you want to give him an opportunity to talk over everyday problems with an individual who has his interests at heart and who is trying to understand him. In explaining this, avoid the use of psychological terms and jargon. If you substitute the term "counseling" for "psychotherapy," your child may be more susceptible to help of this kind. If, after all this, he still says "no," and you have to force him to see the therapist, he may not be ready for help of this kind. Having him undergo treatment when he is so strongly against it could undermine any benefits that he may derive from it.

Help may lie in good old-fashioned strictness and punishment. Should you punish your child and curtail some of his privileges and recreational activities? Should you tell him that even more severe penalties are in store for him unless he buckles down to study and gets better grades? If he has no discipline of his own, you might argue, why not try to impose it upon him from the outside? Naturally, he may not like it at first, but for his own good he will appreciate it in the long run.

This approach, though often frowned upon by the champions of progressive and permissive education, is based on some sound facts about human behavior. It is true that fear, and particularly fear of punishment, motivates and enhances much of our daily behavior. Many people would not work at all if they weren't *afraid* of the consequences.

However, motivation by fear and punishment produces temporary, but rarely lasting, results. Many parents have tried to frighten and punish their children into school work, only to discover that, over a period of time, this approach does not work. Furthermore, if you had been a generally permissive parent in the past, and now try to act tough and demanding, your child will not be able to accept your sudden change of personality and will not take you seriously in your new role as a parent. On the other hand, if you have been a stern and dictatorial parent before, the fact that your child is now failing in school is perfect evidence that there must have been something wrong with your overly strict attitude, and that you may need to change it.

I am not opposed to the application of discipline, and am not advocating a strict "hands-off-your-children" policy. However, I do believe that there are right and wrong kinds of discipline. The most effective kind of discipline is marked by consistency (inconsistency is to promise rewards and punishments that are only rarely carried out). Use a kind but firm and not overtly hostile manner (you don't need to yell and nag continually to be a good disciplinarian).

Though you may be perfectly justified in wanting to apply more discipline to your child to make him study, the particular manner in which you have applied it in the past may have been wrong.

Since discipline at home and home relationships play such an important part in motivating young people's study habits, you may want to re-examine and revise some of your own parental attitudes before you take your child to a therapist, a remedial reading center, or change his school. I am convinced that among all the remedial measures that were discussed so far, this step may be most difficult for you to take, but it may be the most effective one.

194

There is an old saying: "You can lead a horse to water, but you can't make him drink." It is, of course, possible that you may have tried all the suggestions offered here to help your child to become an educated adult, but nevertheless he continues to fail at school. If this is so, you can derive a moderate amount of comfort from the thought that nowadays it is actually never too late for your child to complete his education if he wants to. Even the person who is in his forties or fifties may go to school. The portals of evening colleges or other institutions of higher learning are never locked. In fact, the number of parents and even grandparents who graduate from colleges is increasing every year. With the over-all increase in adult education schools, the opportunity for further study is there at practically any time of life.

Naturally, you would not want such late education for your child, and you should not base all your hope on this future thought, till you have exhausted all the remedial measures presently available. Should you have tried all remedies in vain, realize that education is a life-long process, and that there are quite a few people who can't benefit from it till they are older and more mature. Moreover, it is not uncommon for such individuals to find that special effort and ambition helps them then to compensate for those educational opportunities which they have missed during their childhood and adolescence.

CHAPTER **22** / Friction Between
Adults and Their Parents

Many books and articles have been written about the problems
between young children and adolescents and their parents.
However, it's amazing how little information is available about
the adjustment problems that adults sometimes face in getting
along with their fathers and mothers. This chapter is directed at
you, the grown son or daughter. Perhaps, though you are no
longer as dependent upon your parents as before, you still run
into problems with them.

There seems to be no question in most people's minds that
they love their parents or that they *should* love their parents.
However, despite such good intentions, to what extent you
should love your parents and how you express this love in adult
years often poses a problem.

Perhaps the *first step* in coping with this problem is to recognize that you don't *always* love your parents and you don't
love them unconditionally (if you are really honest with yourself). Yes, you respect them, you feel grateful for what they have
done for you, and you would probably never let them down. But
there must be some moments—as in any love relationship—when
you simply can't stand them and, if not that, when you are at
least irritated by some of their actions. A *second step* is to become more aware of the specific causes of your irritation toward
your parents. You will find some of these causes listed below.

Your parents make demands upon you. Of course such demands are not always obvious. Mother may say, "Do what is best for yourself. Don't let *me* influence you. As long as *you* are happy I am happy." Yet she may be extremely upset if you take this suggestion too literally and ignore her advice completely when you make important decisions in your life. Similarly, if you are a married woman and give your husband all of your devotion but practically none to your Dad, he may not say anything but you could probably tell from the expression on his face that you have hurt him very deeply.

What happens when parental demands are made upon you? If you answer honestly, you feel quite resentful about it. People are willing to give of their time, their money, their attention, and their love, but they get angry when they feel that all this is required of them. Demands made upon you by your parents may therefore deduct from the love you feel for them.

Your parents may have developed certain definite ideas about the kind of person you should be. Expressed in psychological terms, they have built up a certain idealized image of you (perhaps their own unfulfilled childhood ideals). Though you may be allowed to fail them here and there, they expect you to live up to this image. Thus, most mothers want their daughters to be married (sometimes they even specify what kind of man he should be). Similarly, the majority of parents want their sons to be successful. Of course, you yourself want to be successful, yet your ideas of going about it may be quite different from those of your parents. Whether you want to admit it or not, your parents' expectations for you may annoy you quite a bit at times and may also be another reason for your unconsciously disliking them.

You may be emotionally too dependent upon your parents and unwittingly hold this against them. Though they will no longer spank you if you have failed in business or if you can't make a go of your marriage, the fear of their disapproval may make you painfully aware of your dependence upon them. You

197

may *think* you are independent, yet against your better judgment you may buy the house that *they* select, give a name to your child that *they* prefer and, because of *their* opinions, come to resent friends whom you liked previously. It seems that even in adult sons and daughters there is always a streak of rebellion left over from adolescence which has remained sensitive to parental domination. Such smoldering resentment can easily lead to hostile feelings.

Perhaps your affection and love for your parents is dampened at times because you feel that you have outgrown many of their interests and concerns. You do belong to a generation that is different from theirs in many respects, and your parents may often appear old-fashioned to you. Family friction may arise when they stubbornly try to hold onto traditional ideas belonging to their own generation. Thus if you, as a generally responsible person, think nothing of taking a day off from work here and there, your father may not be able to understand this at all. When he was your age, he would rather have contracted pneumonia than stay away from his job for *one single hour*. True, you don't exactly hate your parents for their old-fashioned ideas, yet these ideas can stir nasty and slightly contemptuous thoughts in you.

You yourself may have built up an idealized and unrealistic image of your parents, making it easy for you to become disappointed or angry when they fail to live up to your ideals. Suppose you want your mother to baby-sit for you, but your mother is unable to. Can you *blame* her for not coming? Of course not, because she is not obligated to do this for you. However, you may have such unloving thoughts as these: "What good is Mother anyway when I have to turn to strangers? Why should she not show some consideration after I have given up important things for *her* on previous occasions?" In this instance you are psychologically regressing to the past: you expect the same kind of consideration from your parents as an adult as that which you received as a child.

These reasons for family tension probably appear somewhat trivial and insignificant to you, and perhaps they are. However, add up these sources of irritation, let them pile up over a length of time, and bang, they explode into a big family argument. When that occurs, emotions flare like a fire when small flames have been left to smolder unnoticed. Angry words and emotion-charged accusations are made. Before you know it you feel that your parents don't *understand* you and that you don't understand them.

Now that you have learned some of the reasons *why* you may feel angry or irritated at your parents, here are a few suggestions as to how you can cope with feelings of this kind.

If you are married, don't live with your parents unless financial circumstances make it absolutely necessary. The temptation to "take them in" when they are old and lonely may be strong. However, experience has shown repeatedly that it is extremely difficult for a married man or woman to be a good spouse as well as a good son or daughter under the same roof. The relationships to your parents and to your spouse are emotionally very demanding. To satisfy both simultaneously in a pattern of close and daily living is therefore very hard.

If you are not married, there seem to be many advantages in boarding with your parents. Mother will take care of your laundry, have dinner ready when you come home from work, and be good company when you feel lonely. On the other hand, to spend important years of your adult life under the parental roof also has many disadvantages. Though you may be free to come and go as you please and can invite all your friends to your home, you may remain psychologically tied to the apron strings of your family. Furthermore, it is easy to become so settled and contented under such circumstances that you lose the drive and

199

initiative necessary to establish a *life of your own*. You may shudder, of course, at the thought of living in boarding houses, furnished rooms, and in the loneliness of dingy apartments, but you will often find that you get on better—not worse—with your parents if they are not around all the time.

Define clearly the limits of the parental demands that are made upon you. Of course, some of their demands are justified. Simply because you have outgrown childhood does not mean that you no longer have any obligations to your parents. However, there are certain *limitations* to parental obligations and you should be aware of them. If you are married, the demands made upon you by your wife or husband should take preference over those made by your parents. Draw your mother and father into your family life only as often as you feel you can; let them share in the more important events and decisions; but don't permit them to manage your household, your children, or your life. The same holds true for the single adult. The marital partner you choose, the kind of friends you select, or the kind of job you want should be based on your own decisions, not exclusively those of your parents. As an adult you have a right and *obligation* to look out for yourself and your own benefits as well as those of your parents.

Don't worry if you can't be the ideal *son or daughter.* No matter how hard you try to please your parents, they may sometimes feel that you have not done enough for them. In fact, they may even point out to you how *other*, much better, daughters and sons cater to their parents, sacrifice for them, and spoil them in just about every way. When your parents talk to you this way, just think of the old proverb, "the grass is always greener on the other side of the fence." It is extremely difficult to know what really goes on in the families of other people without actually living with them. Chances are that your parents would not like it at all if they had to live with your neighbors' or friends' sons or daughters. *Their* son may devote each weekend entirely to his mother but may lack some of the other personality traits for which your mother appreciates you.

Just exactly what an *ideal* son or daughter should do for a parent will depend upon the social, economic, and religious background from which he or she comes. The extent to which you still identify with your background will determine what you feel you owe your parents in the way of duty and obligation. However, you don't have to conform in every respect. If, for example, it is customary in your parents' social circles for a son or daughter to come for dinner every Saturday night, but you have commitments of your own, try to reach some compromise. Visit them every other Saturday night or on Sunday. This way you will not give in to all their demands yet you will live up somewhat to their ideal of a "good" son or daughter.

Avoid both excess conformity and unreasonable rebellion. Frances, a woman in her late forties, had never moved away from her home. Furthermore, she spent practically all of her free time with her parents. The family lived in a small community, and Frances worked in a stationery store just a few blocks away from her home. Although she was a bright and capable woman she had always refused jobs that were more remunerative and interesting if they took her away from her immediate home environment. She had had two marriage proposals but turned both of them down because her parents did not approve of the men who wanted to marry her. Although Frances' life was safe and fulfilled in many ways, her sudden depressions and frequent crying spells were manifestations of unconscious frustration and a need for nonparental love and affection.

When she came to me for consultation she expressed

201

much concern about what would happen to her after her parents died, and she voiced regrets about never having had the chance to bear children.

* * *

Harvey was a young doctor who had been the apple of his mother's eye as a child. Later, it was largely because of her efforts and financial sacrifices that Harvey was able to go to medical school. He remained strongly attached to her. While Harvey was living with his mother and attending medical school he became interested in Andrea, a young woman who had rented a furnished room in the house that Harvey's mother owned. Although Harvey was interested in Andrea, he was not really in love with her and had no intention of marrying her. However, he was strongly swayed by his mother's wishes; she thought that Andrea would make an ideal wife for Harvey. Eventually he did marry her. But the marriage worked out poorly in several respects and almost ended in divorce.

After Harvey had been married for a few years, his attitude toward his mother changed completely. He moved away from home. He refused to see her at any time. He did not answer her letters and refused to respond to her telephone calls. Realizing suddenly that he had been over-dependent upon her all his life, he became extremely hostile and belligerent toward her. He tried to cut the umbilical cord by withdrawing from her completely. When Harvey's mother died a few years later, he bitterly regretted what he had done.

Essentially it is the *child* in you that wants to be taken care of even when you are an adult. And it is the *latent adolescent* in you that acts up again when you rebel *excessively* against your parents. Frances had actually never outgrown the childhood

202

dependency which was appropriate when she was younger but which should not have been indulged as an adult. Harvey was reacting like an angry adolescent when he continued to hold a grudge against his mother that may have been justified, but did not have to be carried to such an extreme.

If you don't outgrow infantile dependency upon your parents, you pay with the impoverishment of your own personality and the loss of your initiative. If, as an adult, you continue to act like an angry adolescent toward your father or mother, you create unnecessary friction and arguments. Try to react to your parents with the maturity of an adult and you will be able to establish a sound relationship with them.

Take a new look at your parents. How can you get on with them with a minimum of arguments, only occasional slamming of doors, a minimum of misunderstandings, and with only those hurts and offenses that are absolutely unavoidable?

First of all, try to view them as *individuals,* not purely as your parents. View them objectively, as if they were characters in a novel or a play, characters with whom you do not always agree but whom you find interesting nevertheless—just because they are so different from yourself. Such temporarily objective attitudes toward your parents will give you a new perspective, and might help to reinstate many formerly favorable attitudes toward them that have been marred by too much closeness and obstructed by too many petty details of daily living.

Clarence Day wrote a delightful book called *Life With Father.* In it the author describes many of his father's irritating character traits with genuine love, yet from the point of view of an objective observer. Strange as it may seem, a certain amount of objectivity, distance, and detachment can sometimes promote greater understanding, just as some paintings become clearer and more beautiful when we step a little away from them.

Secondly, capitalize on the many *positive* features of a parental relationship. Keep in mind that you *can* have several friendships, affairs, acquaintances, even wives or husbands, but you have only *one* father or mother. If your parents should die, there is no one to replace them. No matter how bad or annoying your parents may appear to you at times, realize that the source of their attitude is more often genuine concern for you rather than pure selfishness or lasting hate.

Don't forget, too, that you share with your parents many intimate and personal memories of you childhood that others can not easily partake in. To be sure, not all of these memories may be pleasant, but to recall them sometimes with your parents is an enjoyable, unique experience.

Thirdly, don't let the many things that you read about mother-love or father-hate in psychoanalytical literature confuse you. The patterns of relationships that we establish with our parents in childhood may repeat themselves as we grow older but they are never quite the same, and they can be changed and revised if need be.

If *progression* from rather than regression to childhood characterizes your attitude toward your parents as you grow older and as they advance in age, you will discover new common interests, and the sources of trouble and friction will be reduced.

PART FIVE

Helping

Others

in Emotional

Trouble

CHAPTER **23** / Some General Principles

Many people find that playing the role of a guide, adviser, or helper with the emotional problems of others has a strong appeal. In fact, vocational counselors have told me that the desire to become a psychiatrist or psychologist these days is almost as strong as the wish to become a movie star, a baseball hero, or an astronaut.

Unfortunately, the highly responsible and delicate job of helping others with their emotional problems often appeals particularly to those who have many problems of their own. Perhaps this is so because directing the lives of others makes them feel superior, or because they get pleasure from finding that others are even more disturbed than they are. Those who aspire to become psychologists do not realize that, in addition to an intense desire to help others, an understanding attitude and other special skills are required.

Professional therapists and counselors are, of course, not the only ones to help others in emotional distress. In many instances, the right kind of encouragement or advice can be given by a close friend or family member who is not a professional. Such words of emotional wisdom have at times been as helpful as those that come from therapists. The urgency of many everyday emotional problems almost forces the layman into the role of a personal guide and adviser. Not everybody is as cold as the corporal I remember from my Army days. When he was approached by another soldier who wished to get personal advice, the corporal used to say, "If you have a problem go to your chaplain or the psycho ward. Don't ask me to waste my time."

Although I believe that a little knowledge of psychology can often be more dangerous than having none, I think that there are some basic psychological principles in the field of human relationships that can be applied by the layman without doing any harm.

Suppose a family member, or a close friend with a personal problem, needs your help. Are there any ways in which you can improve your "counseling" techniques with the help of modern psychology? I would like to pass on to you some of the knowledge I have gained from my own professional work with people and their problems.

Avoid overinvolvement, and be aware of the importance of gestures and nonverbal communication. In dealing with people who have emotional problems, psychologists have learned that a somewhat neutral and yet warm and perceptive attitude is best. If the troubled person who comes to you is, for example, overanxious and *you* become anxious yourself, he will think his problem is *really* insoluble. On the other hand, he will think you don't really care if your facial expression is too nonchalant. I shall not forget the patient whom I saw during my days of therapeutic training who told me, "Doctor, you always have that smile on your face. It seems as if you're making fun of me. I hate you for feeling so good and carefree!" In an attempt to make the patient feel at ease I had made the mistake of assuming an attitude that reflected *my* general mood but lacked real concern for the patient. Thus the person who comes to you for help will derive clues from your facial expression and your demeanor as to how genuinely concerned you are, and how much you really care.

I might also add here that very often in an emotional crisis, a warm handshake, an embrace, even a casual tap on the shoulder can be more helpful than a barrage of words or empty clichés. Though this is not done in therapy, of course, your more personal relationship with the person who seeks your aid may make it possible. Notice how in movies and theater plays facial expressions and gestures often convey feelings so much more effectively than words.

Avoid premature reassurance. It is very tempting, when others confide in us, to present them with a quick and obvious explanation of their problems, and to use it as a source of reassurance. How many times have you heard such phrases as: it's all in your mind; things are not really so bad; just get a good night's rest and everything will be all right; don't make a mountain out of a molehill; you know you're the greatest guy in the world— buck up.

The trouble with such phrases is that the person to whom they are directed knows only too well that you are oversimplifying matters. If the solution to problems were that easy, your friend would not have needed to approach you in the first place.

Don't cite examples from your own life and your experience. One of the characteristics of emotional distress is that it makes us temporarily more egocentric than we usually are. If you were hit by a car or a fire swept your house, your immediate impulse would be to help yourself. Similarly, in emergencies that are caused by emotional experiences you think of yourself first, and are usually not too interested in what happened to someone else under similar circumstances. For this reason, do not tell the individual who is seeking your emotional support how you went through the same experiences and worse, or elaborate in detail your own troubles and difficulties. That you were able to suddenly pull out of your depression, or that you stopped drinking when you began to see pink elephants on the walls, only makes the troubled person *more* miserable, because in his present state he is unable to foresee how your experiences could happen to *him*. Because you were able to help yourself does not mean that someone else can do the same. Avoid, too, phrases of this kind: I told you so; I knew all the time that you were heading for trouble; when I was in love I went crazy too.

Don't judge or moralize prematurely. Many people who are in personal trouble suffer from feelings of guilt that tear into whatever shreds of self-respect they had. Very often they know only too well that they *should* have acted differently, but something devilish or wild in their natures swept them off their feet.

If you want to help, you are not asked to be and should not try to play the role of judge who sets up the law and dictates what is right and wrong. The girl who is pregnant or has run away from home does not want to be preached to. If you do this, you will only evoke images of angry mothers and fathers who have preached in the past. There is no greater pain than that caused by self-condemnation and guilt. And if you load the weight of additional guilt on the shoulders of an already self-condemning person you can do much harm.

This does not mean, of course, that you should not help people who are confused in their values and morals to straighten these out if necessary. But do not try to do this immediately when the person who comes to you is in acute distress and despair.

Don't get angry if your suggestions are not followed up. A person whose advice is sought can become so enthralled with the sense of his own importance that his pride is hurt severely if his suggestions are not followed.

As a therapist I have learned that the seeds of insight and understanding which have been planted during therapy take long to germinate. If you want to help others with personal problems, it would be presumptuous to think that what you suggest to them can or will be grasped and accepted all at once. Don't be annoyed, therefore, when what you consider pearls of wisdom in the way of advice is at first met with silence or stubborn resistance. Remember that you want to help, not just to find a

210

sounding board for your own opinions, or to prove to yourself how wise and experienced *you* are.

Now that I have outlined some general psychological principles in the following chapters I will apply them to some specific situations.

CHAPTER **24** / Helping the Adolescent

Because many young people want to prove to themselves that they can be self-sufficient and independent, they are often reluctant to accept help and advice from those whom they consider superior to themselves—and parents are often looked at in this way. It is not surprising, therefore, to find that young people don't turn to their parents for advice, but to their peers.

If you are a parent and feel that you would like to help your teenage son or daughter with a problem, you must first earn their complete confidence, but not based upon your authority and the respect owed to you. I have been surprised to discover, in my practice how many young people find it difficult to communicate with or confide in their parents.

If you don't have your son's or daughter's confidence you can admonish, suggest, reassure, or discourage, but it will be of little use. How do you gain their confidence? You must first learn to accept them *as they are*—not as you would like them to be; not as they should be to conform with the standards of your adult friends, and not as you yourself were when you were younger.

To genuinely accept your children as individuals means not only to recognize their good points but also—and this is more difficult—to temporarily accept their faults and shortcomings. Once such acceptance is established, it eventually leads your children to feel the confidence which will enable them to seek your advice or counsel. What has been said here about the establishment of confidence between parents and adolescents also applies, of course, to other interpersonal relationships.

If adolescents turn to you with a personal problem, you must realize that they too are particularly sensitive to certain clichés which have been heard often enough to become meaningless. Such a cliché is the statement, "Wait till you have grown up and everything will be easier." Most young people are impatient, and if you ask them to wait for years until they can solve and understand certain problems you are requesting the impossible.

The term "immaturity" should also be eliminated from your vocabulary if you talk to young people. If you call an adolescent "immature" or imply that he is, you suggest regression to childhood to one who is struggling to become an adult. Though he himself may realize that he is immature in some ways, pointing this out to him will only arouse his antagonism or strengthen his feelings of inadequacy.

Another important consideration is this: When adolescents have emotional problems and are willing to talk to you about them, try to respond to their call for help at once. If you wait too long, or brush off the request for help with such statements as "let's talk about it tomorrow," or "let's discuss it some other time," your best opportunity for being helpful will have passed. Most young people confide most readily and are most open to suggestions at the time when a crisis occurs, not when it is convenient for the person who is trying to do the helping.

In my professional experience I have found that adolescents are most open to suggestions and help in personal crises if they are spoken to and feel accepted at an adult level. As long as the appeal is to the mature aspect of their personalities (there is *some* maturity in every adolescent), they will be willing to give up childish demands and infantile behavior.

CHAPTER **25** / Helping the
Older Person

Who are older people? Books which try to tell the aged that they should be "happy" to be old, put the age limit at about sixty-five, the time when most individuals retire from work. However, age is quite relative. In this connection I am reminded of the ninety-year-old French countess who was asked by a reporter at what age women stop being interested in men. She replied spontaneously, "Why ask me?"

How can you help an older person who needs you or who has approached you with personal problems? Here are some suggestions to help you understand and handle the psychological needs of the aging individual.

Old people need to talk, and like to voice their opinions more strongly than younger individuals. Perhaps it is the aging individual's way of compensating for a progressive slowing down in action. Unfortunately, however, the things that older people talk about are not always interesting to others. They may consist of elaborate complaints about physical ailments, or of events that happened so far in the past that they seem like faded snapshots.

Though I am a great believer in the art of good listening, and have stressed its value in several parts of this book, I don't think it is always wise to just listen to older people and to let

214

them indulge in reminiscence. If done tactfully and without offense, it may be more helpful for you, as a younger person, to stop your old grandmother or grandfather from regressing to the past. Instead, draw them into the present, and refresh them with stories about the things that concern you *now*. They may offer some resistance at first when you tell them about current events or the latest fads and fashions, but in the long run it will be better for them. It could counteract some of the self-centeredness that is sometimes part of the aging process.

Older people want an excessive amount of respect and admiration. You must understand that this is their way of compensating for the loss of prestige and status that sometimes comes with old age. Of course, there may be something in yourself that rebels against the idea of respecting old people *only* because they are more advanced in years than you are. However, try to realize that giving an older person reverence and admiration when it is due does not mean that you lower your own worth or must accept his ideas. Much respect and admiration can be shown in your conduct and general attitude. *Give them the feeling that* you take their judgment and opinions into consideration, but by the same token, *do what you think is right* when it comes to vital decisions in your life. What the aging person cannot accept is to have his advice ignored *entirely*. As long as you are not *completely* deaf to his suggestions he will be satisfied, even though his advice is not always followed.

Older people like presents. We all do, of course. But when you are getting on in years your need for this kind of attention is enhanced. A gift is a tangible symbol of love and care, and it sometimes conveys feelings that cannot be expressed so readily in words. Besides, bringing a gift to the aging individual (it doesn't have to be expensive) can again be an indirect aid in the fight against the dangerous trend of regression into the remote past. Current best-sellers, subscriptions to interesting magazines

215

or newspapers, the reproduction of a modern painting, or a new record make excellent gift items.

Older people want much of your time. If you are young, you may want to spend most of your time with contemporaries who share your current interests and problems more intimately. However, there is no reason why, with careful planning of your activities, you could not set aside an occasional morning, afternoon, or evening to spend with some of the older people who are close to you. When you visit older people, try to be as generous as you can with the time you spend.

Older people tend to become too dependent. It is probably not completely incidental that institutions for the care of the aged are referred to as "nursing" homes. The term "nursing" implies a state of dependence. To adjust to being taken care of again like a child after having been an independent adult is one of the major problems of old age.

As a younger individual, you can do much to help the older person become more independent. Be of assistance, aid, and support whenever you can, but don't do it in the same manner that you would with a helpless infant. Let the aging person do as many things *by himself* as possible. Be ready to move the chair that is in the way, lift the heavy suitcase for him, take over a bothersome errand, but let him first try to do it by himself.

Don't forget that you, too, will be old someday, and whatever you can learn now about the process of adjustment to age may be to your benefit in the future.

CHAPTER 26

Helping the
Severely Disturbed

We are *all* emotionally unstable *to some extent,* or at least have
our neurotic moments. However, just when the diagnostic label
of "neurosis" should be attached to an individual's irrational and
inexplicable behavioral tendencies is often an arbitrary decision.
But situations do arise when a person does demonstrate more
than the usual or commonly accepted amount of emotional upset. When your husband starts drinking to an extent where it
interferes with his career, when you overeat until it becomes a
health hazard, or when depression paralyzes you into inactivity,
the problems involved need special professional attention.

What should you do if such a situation occurs in your family or to one of your friends? Run to the first psychiatrist whom
you can locate in the phone book? Have the person committed
to a mental institution? Only in the case of extreme and dangerous emergencies would it be advisable to take such drastic steps.
It may be wise first to see what you can do *on your own* to alleviate the crisis.

People who have severe emotional problems are *usually
very sensitive about them, and are often reluctant to reveal them
to others.* Thus, the person who takes one drink too many will
often react with a fit of anger if he is told that he is becoming an
alcoholic. A woman who notices homosexual leanings within
herself will refuse to admit them to others.

In coping with the emotional problems that you detect in another person, it would therefore be important for you not to call such problems to his attention, at least for a while, and wait until he is ready to confide in you. Confidence, as was mentioned before, cannot be forced if it is not there in the first place, but it can be developed through an accepting and understanding attitude.

Recently, a case came to my attention in which a woman who had been married for several years was extremely bothered by her husband's inordinate jealousy. He suspected her of having affairs with the mailman, the grocery boy, and practically every male with whom she came in contact. When the husband went to work, he called home constantly to check on what she was doing. Although the woman was desperate and often thought of having her husband "looked over" by a psychiatrist, she kept her faith in him, and met his suspicious accusations firmly but with an attitude of understanding reasonableness and patience. Her wise position paid off in the long run. The man finally explained the grounds for his suspicions. He had received a letter from one of the woman's rejected suitors accusing her of infidelity. Obviously the man who had sent the letter was impelled by a desire for revenge. As soon as the situation was discussed by the married couple it was clarified.

It is a wise policy to wait and be patient before assuming the presence of a serious mental disorder. If you are convinced that there is cause to suspect a severe emotional disturbance in someone you know, try not to label or diagnose it yourself, using psychological or psychiatric terminology. Although you may be certain that a person is hysterical, paranoid, manic, or suffers from a psychosomatic headache, the mere mentioning of such words which are loaded with all kinds of implications will only arouse anger and resentment. If you feel that a person whose behavior concerns you needs psychological or psychiatric care, it may be wise, too, to keep even this to yourself at first. The best

218

you can do under such circumstances is to try to convince the disturbed individual that he has a problem, (not necessarily a psychological one). Instead of at once suggesting therapeutic treatment, consider a visit to a general practitioner who will decide whether there is a need for special psychiatric treatment.

If you feel, however, that the emotional problem encountered is so urgent that it needs immediate psychiatric attention, you could suggest an appointment with a properly qualified mental health clinic, or with a psychiatrist. If you do this it is important to point out that such an appointment serves a merely exploratory purpose and does not necessarily involve future appointments or continued treatment. The essential goal is to get the severely troubled person *to take the first step* toward professional treatment. Once this step is taken, he may be willing to take others. In fact, he may find that the therapist whom he eventually meets is not as "bad" as he thought. He may discover that most so-called headshrinkers are more human and understanding than he was made to believe on the basis of often distorted publicity. It is important to point out here that there are also instances where therapists advise *against* treatment.

Should the individual who needs psychiatric help react to the mere mentioning of the word "psychotherapy" like a bull to a red cloth, consultation with a family service agency may be less threatening or more readily agreed to. If a marital problem is involved, marriage counseling may be a step on the road to help. In some instances also, the idea of *group* therapy may be more acceptable for people who feel that seeing a private therapist is a social stigma.

The proverb that you can lead a horse to water but you can't make him drink also applies to psychotherapy. You can't force a person who is completely opposed to therapeutic treatment to accept it. If such a rigid attitude prevails, try to suggest that reading offers a way to find out more about what therapy is and does. Such books as those written by Lawrence Kubie (*Practical and Theoretical Aspects of Psychoanalysis,* International University Press, 1957), or Rudolph Wittenberg's *Common Sense About Psychoanalysis* (Doubleday, 1962) provide reliable information. Both are available in paperback editions.

A final decision about who needs treatment and who does not should be left to expert professional judgment.

One last thought the statistics that have been compiled about the advantages to be gained from treatment suggest that roughly about two-thirds of patients who undergo psychotherapy have later felt that it helped them considerably.

APPENDIX Reliable sources for
Psychological, Psychiatric, and
Counseling Aid

The list of outpatient clinics published by the National Association for Mental Health.

Your state or local health service.

Your local Community Welfare Counsel of Social Agencies can provide information on counseling services and family group therapy.

Your local medical society can refer you to local psychiatrists or psychologists.

Your state and local Mental Health Association.

Your local Family Service Society.

In states which have certification laws governing psychologists, there is a list of registered psychologists available from the State Education Department.

For a reliable marriage counselor, obtain a referral from your physician or from a psychotherapist.

Agencies which handle very specific problems are listed in the appropriate chapters of this book.